# English Dialectology

# English Dialectology: An Introduction

LAWRENCE M. DAVIS

65918

THE UNIVERSITY OF ALABAMA PRESS

Publication of this book was made possible, in part,
by financial assistance from the Publications
Committee, University of Haifa.

**Library of Congress Cataloging in Publication Data**

Davis, Lawrence M.
  English dialectology.

  Bibliography: p.
  Includes index.
  1. English language—Dialectology. I. Title.
PE1711.D38                     427              81-23164
ISBN 0-8173-0113-5                              AACR2
ISBN 0-8173-0114-3 (pbk.)

# Contents

# Tables and Figures

## Tables

## Figures

# *Preface*

This book is intended primarily as a text for university courses in dialectology and as ancillary reading in introductory linguistics courses. It presupposes an elementary knowledge of phonetics as well as some familiarity with simple terminology. Because it is a textbook, I have avoided footnotes, preferring to list the major sources for chapters 1 and 2 in bibliographical notes at the ends of those chapters. The bibliography, of course, suggests additional reading matter.

My purpose is to survey, critically and objectively, the major work in regional dialectology through 1979 in the United States and in Britain, as well as the basic studies in social dialectology in the United States. This book is thus intended mainly for American students. Insofar as regional dialectology is concerned, the major emphasis is on linguistic atlases rather than on dialect dictionaries such as Frederic G. Cassidy's forthcoming *Dictionary of American Regional English*. Moreover, comparatively little attention has been given to the spate of scholarly articles dealing with specific problems in regional dialectology. A similar procedure has been followed regarding social dialectology; that is, only major works are surveyed here. Most of these are book-length studies, with the exception of the seminal works on Black English and structural dialectology; in these latter cases, many of the major works have, in fact, appeared in article form.

I hope that the reading of this book will stimulate students to read further in the field. For this reason, the bibliography includes, wherever possible, citations of the sources in anthologies that are easily accessible, and where possible in the text I have provided page numbers in these anthologies rather than in the journals where the studies appeared originally.

I should like to thank A. L. Davis, Professor Emeritus of English and Linguistics, Illinois Institute of Technology, and Virginia Glenn McDavid, Professor of English, Chicago State University. They both read the first two chapters, and each made innumerable suggestions, most of which I accepted. Where I did not do so, this book is probably weaker. My thanks also to the University of Haifa, for both its financial support in preparing the maps and for a peaceful sabbatical year in the United States that permitted me to write.

There is no adequate way to thank my wife, Nurit, for her patience during the writing of this book and for bearing far more than her share of taking care of Maya, Jonathan, and Michael.

Permission to reproduce copyrighted material is gratefully acknowledged to publishers and authors as follows:

Maps from *A Survey of Verb Forms in the Eastern United States*, by E. Bagby Atwood, copyright © 1953 by The University of Michigan Press. Used by permission.

Maps from *A Word Geography of the Eastern United States*, by Hans Kurath, copyright © 1949 by The University of Michigan Press. Used by permission.

Tables from *Variation and Change in Alabama English*, by Crawford Feagin, copyright © 1979 by Georgetown University Press, Washington, D.C. Used by permission.

Map from *Grease and Greasy—A Study of Geographical Variation*, by E. Bagby Atwood, in *Studies in English* (Volume XXIX), copyright © 1950 by The University of Texas Press. Used by permission.

Figures and map from *The Linguistic Atlas of the Upper Midwest*, by Harold B. Allen, copyright © 1973, 1975, 1976 by The University of Minnesota. Used by permission from The University of Minnesota Press.

Map from *The Pronunciation of English in the Atlantic States*, by Hans Kurath and Raven I. McDavid, Jr., copyright © 1961 by The University of Michigan Press. Used by permission.

Maps from *Phonological Atlas of the Northern Region: The Six Northern Counties, North Lincolnshire and the Isle of Man*, by Eduard Kolb, copyright © 1964 by Franke Verlag. Used by permission.

Maps from *A Word Geography of England*, by Harold Orton and Nathalia Wright, copyright © 1974 by Seminar Press. Used by permission.

Passages from *Handbook of the Linguistic Geography of New England*, by Hans Kurath, et al., copyright © 1939 by The American Council of Learned Societies. Used by permission.

Tables reprinted with permission of Macmillan Publishing Co., Inc., from *Statistical Methods for Research Workers*, by R. A. Fisher, 14th edition, copyright © 1970 by University of Adelaide.

Map from *Linguistic Atlas of England*, edited by Harold Orton, Stewart Sanderson, and John Widdowson, copyright © 1978 by Croom Helm Ltd. Reprinted by permission.

Map and description from *Linguistic Atlas of Scotland*, by J. Y. Mather and H. H. Speitel, copyright © 1975 by Croom Helm Ltd. Used by permission.

Tables and figures from *The Social Stratification of English in New York City*, by William Labov, copyright © 1966 by Center for Applied Linguistics. Used by permission.

Figures from *A Sociolinguistic Description of Detroit Negro Speech*, by Walter A. Wolfram, copyright © 1969 by Center for Applied Linguistics. Used by permission.

Tables and figure from *Appalachian Speech*, by Walter Wolfram and Donna Christian, copyright © 1976 by Center for Applied Linguistics. Used by permission.

Figures from "Is a Structural Dialectology Possible?" by Uriel Weinreich, in *Word* 10, copyright © 1954 by International Linguistic Association.

# English Dialectology

# 1

## *Some Basics*

### Dialect and Language

Before we begin to talk about dialectology, we should first define *dialect* itself. In fact, the term has several meanings. The French talk about *French* on the one hand and the *dialects* of French on the other; here the term refers to varieties (we shall soon call them *nonstandard* varieties) of a language which are, in this case, spoken beyond the confines of Paris. Generally, this is the definition of *dialect* with which most of us are familiar. It is not the one used by linguists, but it does suggest the attitude of the French toward their language.

Linguists start with the assumption that all human beings speak their own *idiolects*. Similar idiolects make up a particular dialect, and similar dialects make up a particular language. This statement in some sense presupposes that all the idiolects of a dialect and all the dialects of a language are mutually intelligible, but such is not always the case. A Cockney taxi driver in London might have considerable difficulty understanding a farmer from the backwoods of eastern Kentucky, and both the farmer and the taxi driver might have trouble understanding a fisherman from Maine. To an even greater extent a member of the upper class of Venice would find almost incomprehensible the lower-class speech of Sicily.

On the other hand, the distinction between languages is also not particularly clear if we use mutual intelligibility as a criterion. For example, a native speaker of Danish can understand Norwegian, even though Danish and Norwegian are always considered different languages. People from near Kiev insist that they speak Ukrainian, not Russian, although the two "languages" are mutually intelligible. For these and other

reasons, then, we cannot use the test of mutual intelligibility to differentiate between *dialect* and *language*, at least not in any strictly scientific
sense.

Another problem with our definition concerns the word *similar*. If
similar idiolects can be grouped into dialects and similar dialects into
languages, we clearly need some rigorous definition of *similar*. We will
return to this problem in chapter 4 ("The Search for a Structural Dialectology"), but for now it is sufficient to say that such a definition does not
exist.

If we decide to be somewhat less than completely scientific, however,
the test of mutual intelligibility can carry us a long way. In the case of the
speakers from London, Kentucky, and Maine, even though they have
difficulty in understanding each other, all know that the language
spoken is English. The Dane who can understand Norwegian can do so
because the Danes once conquered Norway and ruled there for a long
time and because both Danish and Norwegian were themselves once
dialects of the same parent language—North Germanic. One reason why
we speak today of two different languages is the political boundary
between them. The case of the Ukrainians is somewhat more complex.
To any Slavic linguist, the dialects spoken near Kiev are dialects of the
Russian language; however, Ukrainian nationalism is such that the
Ukrainians themselves, proud of their traditions, say that they speak a
language different from Russian.

The fact is that there is no very clear distinction today between the
terms *dialect* and *language*, or at least no distinction which will bear the
test of severe scientific scrutiny. We have seen that different languages
are sometimes mutually intelligible and that dialects, so defined, of the
same language are sometimes not mutually intelligible at all. Our problem is simplified enormously, however, if we turn to the speakers themselves. We have already seen that the English speakers from Kentucky,
London, and Maine all feel that they speak English. Norwegians say that
they speak Norwegian, Danes Danish, and Ukrainians Ukrainian.
Hence, for our purposes here, if people say that they speak language *x*,
then they do.

In the English-speaking world, unquestionably because of the pejorative connotations associated with the term, few people will admit that
they themselves speak a *dialect* of English; that term we reserve for
people who talk differently from the way we do. Even in this respect
speakers of English use the term *accent*, and indeed one can hear discussions about the accents of people from New York, London, and so on.
But *accent*, from the dialectologist's point of view at least, is not sufficiently descriptive, since the word suggests that dialects differ in terms
of pronunciation only. In fact, they differ in other ways as well. To *knock*

*up* a woman in London is to awaken her; in New York it is to impregnate her. *Garbagemen* in New York are *dustmen* in London. An American automobile has a *trunk*; an English automobile has a *boot*. Similarly, some speakers of English say *he do*, while other, better educated ones say *he does*. So *accent* simply does not seem to be descriptive enough to cover all the facts of language and of dialectal variation.

Dialects differ in three ways: pronunciation (*phonology*), vocabulary (*lexicon*), and grammar. Since the term *dialect* itself has become a carrier of negative connotations, some linguists have argued that the term *variety* should be used instead. Certainly *variety of language* carries no opprobrium and may therefore be better. On the other hand, there seems no real reason for abandoning the term *dialect* once we strip from it the pejorative connotations. For our purposes a dialect is simply a variety of a language, within the limits already noted. Everyone, in other words, speaks a dialect. The French, or for that matter the general English, use of the term *dialect* is not the one which we shall adopt here. For us, *dialect* and *variety* will be understood as completely synonymous, and we can interpret the French sense of *dialect* to mean that some dialects are more prestigious than others. In the case of the French language community, the upper-class dialect of Parisian French is *standard*, while the dialect of, for example, Normandy is nonstandard. This subject will be discussed below in more detail, in the section of this chapter on social dialects.

## Regional Dialects

Many reasons have been given for the origin of dialect differences, and perhaps the most intriguing of all are those which purport to account for dialect differences in the realms of physiology or meteorology. In the United States, for example, it was once fashionable to argue that American black people spoke differently from whites because the former have "thicker lips" and "lazier tongues" than the latter. Since there are in the United States many blacks whose speech is indistinguishable from that of whites, such a statement is clearly preposterous. There seem to be no physiological differences between the races which are reflected in speech. Although the Chinese and other Mongoloid peoples have differently shaped incisors, a Caucasoid child brought up in China among the Chinese will speak Chinese as a native speaker, even if both the child's parents spent their whole lives in Chicago, Illinois.

The climatic explanation for dialect differences is almost more fascinating than the physiological one, mainly because it is more widely held. Many Americans believe that the so-called southern drawl is a function of the hot weather in the southern United States. The weather is so hot, the explanation goes, that people get tired easily and consequently speak more slowly. Still, coastal South Carolinians do not speak slowly at all; moreover, a language such as Vietnamese, spoken (among other places) in the jungles of that country, is spoken at a very rapid tempo. Raven I. McDavid writes: "A professor of pedagogics at the University of Colorado once declared that Minnesotans nasalize their speech because of the damp climate; Eric Partridge has repeatedly attributed the supposed nasalization of Australian speech to the excessively dry climate" (McDavid 1958:483). Since diametrically opposite climates are here taken as explanations of the same phenomenon—nasalization—it seems clear that we must look elsewhere for the reasons for dialect differences.

The reasons for dialect differences are certainly many, so it is fruitless to search for one explanation, as some people have done in the past, for their development and maintenance. Rather, there is a complex of reasons. First, however, it is important to note that, as far as we know, there have always been dialects. Aristophanes made fun of dialects of Greek different from his own; Catullus, writing in Latin, did the same. Old English, spoken 1,300 years ago, had at least four major dialects, each of which had more minor ones. In other words, it is a serious mistake to consider today's dialects as somehow corruptions of some purer form of a language. They are, rather, one of the many aspects of language, and we can at least examine some of the factors which contribute to dialect variation.

Perhaps the most commonly cited reason for the development and maintenance of dialects is *geography*. Although one can overstress the importance of this factor, there seems no question that, particularly in the days before mass communication, a river like the Ohio, a chain of mountains like the Alleghenies, or an impassable desert would keep peoples apart, and it is axiomatic in dialectology that the isolation of peoples breeds linguistic development along different lines. In the Pacific, for example, the various island languages, such as Maori, Fiji, and Hawaiian, were once dialects of the same language; however, continued isolation resulted in their becoming separate languages. In the Middle East and North Africa, to take another case, the different dialects of today's spoken Arabic can be attributed in large measure to past difficulties in communication in that area.

Another factor is the existence of *political boundaries*. In the time before mass communication, the diocesan boundaries and the Danelaw in England were major lines of demarcation, and those lines had been unchanged for centuries. Therefore it is not particularly surprising that many of today's English dialects are still differentiated to some extent along these old political boundaries.

A major influence on the development of dialects is the phenomenon of *immigration*. As new waves of immigrants came to the United States, American English underwent significant changes. In fact, the dialect areas of North America reflect, to a large extent, the settlement history of the area. In Israel there are two major dialects of Hebrew, each representing one of the two major groups of Jews who have settled there: at least as far as its inventory of phonemes is concerned, one dialect is basically Indo-European, and its speakers are in large measure the descendants of European immigrants; the other contains some sounds which are still common in Arabic but which are absent from the European variety, and it is spoken by the descendants of immigrants from the Moslem countries of North Africa and the Middle East.

The last factor which will concern us here is that of *territorial conquest* and its consequences. The victory of William of Normandy at the Battle of Hastings in 1066 meant that for some several centuries French was the "official" language of England, and of course today's English vocabulary reflects that influence. The French were far stronger in the south of England, however, and some of the differences between southern and northern dialects today are attributable, in part at least, to the fact that northern dialects were not so heavily influenced by French.

These four factors—geography, political boundaries, immigration, and territorial conquest—are not the only forces operating to create and/or maintain language variety. They are certainly significant, however, and usually a combination of them is at work. It should be noted further that none of these factors is linguistic in any sense of the word. They are essentially nonlinguistic, but they have far-reaching linguistic consequences. Moreover, we noted that dialects are not corruptions of some purer language. In the next section we shall take up a further aspect of this question: socially meaningful language variation. Here, too, we shall see that the major criteria for determining or identifying a *standard dialect* are also nonlinguistic. That is, we find that dialectology itself must be seen as overlapping other disciplines, such as anthropology, history, and sociology. The dialectologist studies language using the principles of linguistics and other fields and in doing so helps us to understand that complex creature who, in his audacity, called himself *Homo sapiens*.

## Social Dialects: The Concept of a Standard Dialect

Once we are aware of the problems and pitfalls involved in the definition of *dialect*, we can define a *social dialect* as that variety of a language which is spoken by a definable social class: poor people in Appalachia, the Detroit upper middle class, and so on. Once we define *social dialect* in this manner, we immediately see that in most societies there are higher and lower social classes, and therefore we can also assume that there are some social dialects which are more prestigious and others, of course, which are less so. Similarly, as I suggested in the preceding section, there are in many countries cultural centers which exert profound influence on the political, economic, and linguistic life of those countries.

If we consider together the influence of social classes and that exerted by cultural centers, we can arrive at a characterization of the concept *standard dialect*. We noted in the preceding section that speakers of French discriminate between French, the upper-class dialect of Paris, on the one hand, and *dialects of French* on the other. Although this is not our own definition of *dialect*, the distinction does tell us that the most prestigious variety of French is that of the upper class of Paris. In other words, we can characterize the variety of French spoken by the Parisian upper class, in our own terms now, as the *standard dialect* of French. Furthermore, it is not difficult to understand how and why this dialect became standard. For centuries Paris has been the cultural, economic, and political center of France, and it is but natural that the language of that city should exert an influence equal to the city's importance in other realms as well.

A similar situation exists in Italy. As a result of the importance of Florence, particularly during the Renaissance, the standard Italian dialect, even today, is the dialect of upper-class Florentines. Although Rome has to a great extent superseded Florence in the areas of political and economic influence, Italians still look to Florence as the cultural center of the Italian-speaking world. In this case, and in the case of French as well, the label *standard dialect* is not given to a particular variety of a language by the dialectologist; rather, the dialectologist simply describes a situation which already exists in a particular society. That is, the society itself, for various historical reasons, may "choose" one dialect in preference to all the others, and such a dialect is often that of the upper class in a cultural center.

As is the case with most things linguistic, however, the situation in most parts of the world is not as simple as that described for Italy and France. The *Hochdeutsch* (High German) of today was in medieval times only one of the many dialects of what we now call Old High German, a language with many dialects but without any standard one. The Hochdeutsch of today is in many ways a combination of several dialects, and German speakers will often say that it is the dialect spoken in and around Hannover. It has been suggested that Martin Luther's Bible helped considerably to fix this dialect as a recognized standard within the German-speaking community, but clearly the process was already well under way in Luther's time. Today, speakers of German recognize Hochdeutsch as standard, and people who live in places such as Switzerland, Austria, and, for that matter, Berlin generally use the standard dialect for formal purposes, preferring their local dialects for more informal occasions.

The situation in England is still more complicated. During the years before the Norman invasion of England, there were basically four dialects of what was then Old English: Northumbrian, Kentish, Mercian, and West Saxon (see figure 1–1). West Saxon, and not Mercian (the dialect of London), was the standard dialect of English in the year 950, and a look at the political and economic situation at the time can tell us why. The court of the kings of England, until the ascension of William I in 1066, was at Winchester, in the heart of the West Saxon dialect area. Most formal documents and other important writing were in the West Saxon dialect, when, of course, they were not in Latin.

Between the Old English period and that of Middle English (the time of Geoffrey Chaucer), a space of some 500 years, profound changes had taken place in the political and economic life of the English, and these changes are reflected in equally profound linguistic developments. The main point to concern us here, of course, is that during that period the crown moved from Winchester to London. Standard English, by Chaucer's time (c. 1340–1400), had already changed, being no longer the dialect of the upper class of Winchester but that of the upper class of London, and the dialect of Winchester had become more provincial. Chaucer wrote and spoke London English, but then Chaucer, though born in Ipswich, was in fact a Londoner. Even more interesting for our purposes is the fact that John Wycliffe, a Yorkshireman, also wrote in London English when he did his translation of the Bible. Literature in other dialects was still being written during this period, but London's linguistic preeminence was already a fact by 1400.

The development of movable type in the 1450s meant that English spelling began to be standardized. As is the case with all languages, however, the spoken language continued to develop. Until the middle years of the twentieth century, upper-class London English maintained its status as the standard dialect, not just of England, but of the whole of Britain and most of the English-speaking world, excluding North America. In fact, the phonology of that standard dialect was so prestigious that the great English phonetician and linguist Daniel Jones was able to call it *received pronunciation*, or, quite simply, *RP*. It was the dialect of people who sent their sons to one of the two universities, Oxford or Cambridge, and hence was sometimes called *Oxbridge*. It was the dialect of the British Broadcasting Corporation (BBC). It was *the* standard. Anyone who was not a Londoner of the right class and who wanted to succeed in a large

*Figure 1–1*. The Dialects of Old English.

London business or in the civil service had to change his local dialect, in formal situations at least, to make it conform to the London standard, to RP.

During the middle years of the twentieth century, this situation began to change somewhat. By the 1960s people apparently began to take greater pride in their local dialects and thereby to relegate less prestige to the upper-class London dialect. By the mid-1970s, one could hear local dialects from even the BBC. There are as many explanations for this phenomenon as there are Englishmen, but perhaps the most intriguing holds that the Beatles, speaking their Liverpool dialect, influenced English linguistic attitudes every bit as much as they influenced attitudes about music and the length of men's hair. Such explanations are unquestionably interesting, amusing, and thought-provoking but are probably not valid. As was the case with Luther's Bible, we can be fairly certain that other, more pedestrian forces were already at work long before the chaps from Liverpool came on the scene. In any case, if current trends continue, the Englishman of the twenty-first century may not recognize any particular dialect as standard. On the other hand, RP still maintains much of its prestige, and predictions in matters linguistic have never been particularly accurate. Only the passage of time will provide the answers.

When we turn to the English spoken in the United States and Canada, we find a situation that in some respects resembles that of the German-speaking world of the Middle Ages, although of course North Americans are more mobile than were medieval men and women. The fact is that no one city or area dominates the political, economic, and cultural life of North America, and therefore no one dialect is recognized as standard by the society at large. Such a situation, in the United States at least, has not resulted in a more democratic attitude toward language variation, however. Quite the opposite situation exists today, in fact, and we can look at what can be called the *mythology of American English* to understand the situation better.

There is widespread belief in the United States that some kind of general standard dialect exists for the whole of the country and that this variety of English is devoid of all regional markings. Often, in fact, people argue that their own variety of English is the standard, especially if they come from the northern Middle West. The linguistic realities in the United States are far more complex than this mythology. There are numerous cultural centers throughout the country, and each exerts influence of one kind or another on the speech of the surrounding area. One sort of influence is negative. That is, Americans living in rural areas have traditionally tended to distrust "city folk" and often mock the speech of the nearest city. Such a situation existed until fairly recently in the area surrounding Cincinnati, Ohio. On the other hand, the city can exert a positive influence, and such is generally the case in the United States. For example, Richmond, Virginia, has exerted a linguistic influence on the neighboring area such that the workers of the *Linguistic Atlas of the Middle and South Atlantic States* were able to trace the spread of city forms into the countryside.

In the United States and Canada, at least as far as pronunciation is concerned, we find not one standard but many, and there is no one pronunciation of American English which is "acceptable" to all North Americans. This fact means, of course, that a highly educated person from Boston or Atlanta will "sound strange" to a member of his own social class in New Orleans or Toronto. It was noted earlier that "everyone speaks a dialect," and nowhere is this more evident than in the speech of North Americans.

For example, the cultivated speaker in Cleveland and Chicago will "pronounce the /r/" in words like *car, far*, and *barn*. This pronunciation, however, marks a speaker in places like Charleston, South Carolina, as uncultivated or lower class. The very speech form which marks the speaker as upper class on his home ground, then, may mark him as lower class somewhere else.

In the realm of grammar, on the other hand, the situation is far less complex; there does exist, for all intents and purposes, a standard grammar for the whole of North America. With some very few exceptions in spoken discourse (some cultivated coastal Southerners do use verb forms such as *he might could've done that*), all cultivated speakers of North American English use the same grammatical forms. *I seen you last night* is nonstandard everywhere, whereas the social implications of "leaving off an /r/" are a function of where the speaker lives.

One further point must be made about American English dialects. Whether spoken in the United States or in Canada, American English is certainly neither a corruption of British English nor a kind of archaic British English. Although some Englishmen such as Sir Denis Brogan have written about "the horrible American English" (*Spectator*, February 14, 1970), American English is surely viable. And it is not merely "slang." The beginnings of American English were certainly auspicious, since the language brought to the American colonies was no less than the variety of English spoken at the time of Shakespeare—known today as Early Modern English. Although many English dialects were spoken by those first settlers, American English has developed in many ways different from those of its parent. Moreover, many Canadians owe their linguistic roots to their ancestors, loyal to George III, who left the colonies during the Revolution. Today, just as many Englishmen regard with some ambivalence the various American dialects, so also is there a real sense in the United States, and even in Canada, that British dialects, and even RP itself, may be clearly "foreign." As noted earlier, it is axiomatic that isolation breeds different linguistic development, and no better proof of this phenomenon can be found than in the case of the English spoken in North America, in both its standard and its nonstandard varieties.

## Social Dialects: The Concept of a Nonstandard Dialect

Since everyone in the world speaks a dialect, and since some of them are standard, it only stands to reason that many are nonstandard. That is, for every standard variety of a language there are several nonstandard ones. In the case of French, anyone who does not speak the dialect of the Parisian upper class speaks nonstandard French. Anyone who does not speak Hochdeutsch does not speak standard German. Anyone who does not speak upper-class Florentine Italian speaks a nonstandard dialect of Italian. In all these cases, and in many more not discussed here, the *culture*, the society in which a particular language is spoken, determines which dialect is standard and which ones are not so.

To make this distinction, however, we need to have a fairly clear notion of the concept *culture* itself. One definition of many, but that which best suits our purposes here, says that culture is *the sum total of one's learned behavior*. This definition sounds simple enough until we realize that just about everything we do has been learned: the way we talk, stand, or sit, the distance we stand apart while talking, how we use our hands during speech, and, for that matter, even the ways we make love. All of us have a sense of smell, it is true, but the culture in which a person lives teaches him to react positively to one odor and negatively to another. It is also worth noting that such reactions, the result of learned behavior, are seldom recognized as anything but totally "natural." Seldom do we realize that *our* way of looking at the world around us, taught by our culture, is not the only way. It seems natural to us, so we assume that it is natural for everyone.

Some examples might be useful. In what may be called generally *European culture* (the French certainly differ from Americans, but both have more in common than either does, for example, with the mountain people of Tibet), an adult speaking very loudly may be considered crude or boorish. In another culture, that same person might be considered assertive and a natural leader. In European culture, meals end with dessert, often something sweet. A formal dinner in China ends with a light soup, and sweets may be eaten during the dinner. European languages have a very limited number of words which describe smells: something can smell sweet, sour, good, bad. In Totonac, an American

Indian language, there are at least nineteen different words for olfaction: the smells of flowers or food, of mushroom mold, of leather or sweat, and so on.

Since these various kinds of cultural behavior exist, and since individuals consider their way of doing things to be the "natural" way, it is no wonder that we tend to place labels on behavior which is different from our own. Depending on who is doing the judging, Americans are either overly familiar or simply friendly; Germans are either authoritarian or well mannered and orderly; the Japanese are either sly or clever; the English are either dull or dependable. We tend to view the behavior of people from other cultures through the glass of our own, as if we ourselves were behaving that way. Englishmen and, to a somewhat lesser extent, Americans shake hands upon meeting. Japanese males in the traditional society would not touch each other at all, and Latin-American males greet their friends by embracing them. This difference does not mean that the Japanese are standoffish or that Latin Americans are effusive. Things simply look a certain way when we view the behavior of others through the lens of our own culture. An anthropologist, on the other hand, would know that these are three different ways to greet a friend, the particular form being determined by the culture involved.

Since most of us are not anthropologists, we tend to react more simply. If, for example, our culture teaches us that Germans are humorless and authoritarian, and if our personal experience is limited to the extent that we have encountered no contradictory evidence, then how might we react to someone speaking German or, for that matter, English with a German accent? The natural reaction is clearly that the person speaking is likewise humorless and authoritarian. The language of the person triggers what we may call a *stereotypic response*. As a general rule, when we react positively or negatively to a person's speech, it is not really the language but the culture or subculture the person represents which either pleases or offends us—not the language but the individual which we either find pleasant or reject. We know, of course, that every Frenchman or Italian is not romantic or a great lover, but if our cultural mythology teaches us that they are so, then a speaker of Italian or French may trigger in us that stereotypic response.

Although this discussion of the relationship between language and culture has been over simplified, it should provide us with enough background to understand better the question of nonstandard dialects. We saw earlier that any dialect of French which is not upper-class Parisian is not standard. What does that fact mean for the speaker of nonstandard French? The answer is quite simple, since Parisians generally regard anyone not living in Paris as "provincial." Regardless of the actual sophistication of a person from, for example, Normandy or Casablanca, language, a given local dialect, can trigger that stereotypic response in the Parisian and may do so to the extent that a less qualified Parisian may be hired in preference to a more qualified person from somewhere else. Again, the problem is not the *dialect* but rather the fact that certain places are regarded as provincial, where people are unsophisticated and, generally, "not as good as we are." Similarly, in the United States, where there exists a considerable amount of distrust and tension between the races, a voice over the telephone, in answer to a newspaper advertisement of a rental apartment or requesting a reservation at a restaurant or hotel, may trigger a negative response. In fact, many white Southerners have had considerable difficulty doing business over the telephone in northern American cities. Their southern speech forms identified them to their listeners as black. Some found that the only way to rent an apartment or make a reservation at a hotel or restaurant was either to go to the places in person or to ask a northern friend to make the call.

What kinds of options are open to a person who speaks a nonstandard dialect? For the person from Normandy or Casablanca, the solution is comparatively simple: since almost everyone in the French language community recognizes the prestige value of standard French, one must learn that variety of the language if one wants to compete in the marketplace with other standard speakers. In doing so, however, since language and culture are so closely intertwined, the person from Normandy or Casablanca tacitly recognizes the superiority of Parisian *culture* as well.

The American from the South could learn a variety of standard northern English, but in the American case the problem is far more complex. We noted earlier that no one dialect of American English is standard everywhere on the North American continent. What, then, happens to a white speaker of, for example, the standard dialect of Atlanta who moves northward to Chicago? To begin with, he or she might well encounter difficulties such as those noted above. On the other hand, in a liberal community such as that surrounding the University of Chicago, southern speech forms might just as easily trigger the stereotypic response that the speaker is a bigot. The dialect which was completely standard in Atlanta, then, becomes a distinct liability in Chicago and, for all practical purposes, may be considered nonstandard there. Unlike speakers of nonstandard French, however, Atlantans do not accept the speech and the culture of Chicago as somehow superior to their own; hence what they do linguistically can have serious psychological ramifications. If someone from Atlanta decides to conform more with the Chicago standard, that person must of necessity reject part of his or her home culture. If the Atlantan decides against doing so, he or she may face the problems noted above. In any case, the decision will not be a good one.

One alternative suggested by some linguists is *functional bidialectalism*. This solution means that a person changes his or her language to meet new situations in much the same way that we dress differently for different occasions. In this way, changes in one's language are made for purely pragmatic reasons that do not involve the kinds of value judgments noted above. If we carry the clothes analogy further, we can see that a battered tee shirt might be considered sloppy by some people, but the owner of the tee shirt might consider it simply comfortable, to be worn at home and at other informal occasions. One would not wear it at an interview for a position in the U.S. Department of State. So also with changes that a person may make in his or her language.

## Conclusion and Summary

We have seen that the commonly accepted definition of *dialect* as some kind of "corruption" of a pure language is not appropriate for us. In fact, there are fundamental problems involved in trying to differentiate between the terms *language* and *dialect* in any scientific or rigorous sense. We settled finally on what we may call a *sociolinguistic* definition: if people say they speak language *x*, then they do, and we accept the situation as so defined. We also noted that dialects differ in three ways: in phonology, in lexicon, and in grammar. The origin of dialects, we say, is mainly a function of history and geography rather than the result of climatic conditions or human physiology.

The concept *standard dialect*, like the distinction between *language* and *dialect*, must be social in nature. In a particular society, for a variety of economic, political, and cultural reasons, one dialect usually emerges as the standard, and we can identify such standards by turning to the upper classes in major cultural centers. Another important clue is the dialect of a language to which people switch from their native dialects when such people try to advance professionally. We also noted that the standard dialect of one time need not always remain so, as happened with English from the Old English period to the Middle English period of Chaucer. Similarly, as far as phonology is concerned, there is no one regional dialect which is standard for all of North America.

The problems involved in the description and understanding of the phenomenon of nonstandard dialects, no less than those involving standard ones, are tied closely to the concept *culture*, the learned behavior of man. Our culture, whatever it may be, teaches us to react in certain stereotypic ways toward the speech of others. If that reaction is positive for the culture as a whole, then generally no social problems result. If, on the other hand, prejudices exist in a society, and such prejudices are probably universal, then a nonstandard dialect identified with a group against which those prejudices are directed can result in a person's speech being detrimental to the fulfillment of his or her intellectual potential. In any case, the responsibility of the dialectologist engaged in research, whether it is regional or social in its emphasis, must be to describe the linguistic and the social facts as objectively as possible. These facts, though not of the researcher's making and often unpleasant to confront, are part and parcel of the linguistic situation in a particular society. The description of these facts is known as dialectology, and in the following chapters we shall take a closer look at research predicated on the principles outlined here. We shall see that the principle of objectivity is the main one, the measure against which all dialectology, and for that matter all science, is judged.

## Bibliographical Note

For a general introduction to the question of dialect versus language, see Sapir (1921, 1931) and McDavid (1958, 1966). A. L. Davis (1972a) and Hall (1959, 1966) are the main sources for the discussion of culture.

# 2

# *Regional Dialectology*

## The Beginnings in Europe

English dialectology, in a very real sense, owes many of its methods and goals to the origins of modern dialectology in Europe during the last quarter of the nineteenth century. In both Germany and France, scholars began to take an interest in dialects, and we can better understand the more recent work in Britain and in North America if we first examine this earlier work on the Continent.

In 1876, four events took place in the German-speaking world which were to have a profound effect on the future, not just of dialectology, but of all linguistics as well. The first of these events was the publication of Eduard Sievers's *Grundzüge der Lautphysiologie* ("Principles of the Physiology of Speech"). This work, which in later editions was called *Grundzüge der Phonetik* ("Principles of Phonetics"), helped greatly to develop the science of phonetics, one of the basic tools of dialectology. The second event was the appearance of *Die Kerenzer Mundart des Kantons Glarus* ("The Speech of Kerenzen, in the Canton of Glarus [Switzerland]"), written by Jost Winteler, a student of Sievers who used his master's technique of detailed phonetic analysis for the first time. Winteler's methodology was used for fifty years as the basic model for the study of dialects and was superseded only during the second quarter of the twentieth century. The third event was to have even wider significance than the first two: the emergence of the idea that languages change historically in perfectly orderly ways and that sound *laws* can be written to describe those changes. This position was greatly influenced by Sievers's work and found expression in studies by the *Junggrammatiker* ("Neogrammarians"): Karl Brugmann, August Leskien, Hermann Paul, and others. They held that sound laws admit of no exceptions, and it is worthwhile to take a moment to understand what they meant.

Jacob Grimm, although he is better known today for the folk tales that he and his brother Wilhelm collected, studied the relationship between the reconstructed language called *Indo-European*, the parent language of most of the European languages (but not Finnish or Hungarian), Persian, and even Hindi, and the reconstructed language called *Germanic*, the parent of German, English, Swedish, and many others. This is not the place to discuss linguistic reconstruction; for our purposes it is sufficient to note that Grimm found that regular changes had occurred within the phonologies of the two languages as Germanic developed from Indo-European and that these changes could be easily described. The following is *Grimm's Law*:

| *Indo-European* | | *Germanic* | | |
|---|---|---|---|---|
| bh | → | β | → | b |
| dh | → | ð | → | d |
| gh | → | ɣ | → | g |
| p | → | f | | |
| t | → | θ | | |
| k | → | x | (h initially) |
| b | → | p | | |
| d | → | t | | |
| g | → | k | | |

In other words, the aspirated voiced stops eventually lost their aspiration, the voiceless stops became fricatives, and the nonaspirated voiced stops became voiceless. There were some cases which were not covered by Grimm's Law, however, and it took the Danish scholar Oskar Verner to discover a corollary to Grimm's Law which covered the major exceptions. This so-called sound law was believed to be regular, to occur in every word in which the relevant sounds occurred, and the doctrine of *Ausnahmslosigkeit der Lautgesetze* ("immutability of sound change") dominated European linguistics for several decades.

During these same years, it was generally accepted that the best place to see the process of sound change, immutable as it was supposed to be, was in the nonstandard dialects of a language. The last of the four events of 1876, Georg Wenker's work on German dialects, began in the Rhineland, and the main goal of his research at that time was to demonstrate the validity of the theory of the immutability of sound change. Wenker mailed a questionnaire containing thirty-eight short sentences in standard German to 1,266 schoolmasters in the Rhine Valley and asked them to "translate" the sentences into the local dialect. The schoolmasters must have returned the questionnaires with a speed uncharacteristic for academics, because one year later, in 1877, Wenker was able to publish his results as *Das rheinische Platt* ("Low German of the Rhine Valley").

After he received government support, Wenker revised the Rhine Valley questionnaire to include forty sentences containing a total of 339 words. Typical sentences included: "In winter, dry leaves blow in the wind" and "Our mountains are higher than yours." In addition to the transcription of the sentences in local dialect, Wenker asked each schoolmaster to note the name and place of birth of each informant. The questionnaire was sent to Westphalia in 1877, to the rest of the north and middle Germany in 1879, and to the rest of the German empire in 1887. The response was staggering from any point of view. Wenker received a total of 44,251 responses from 40,736 communities.

The problems with such a questionnaire should be obvious. We should remember that phonetics as a modern discipline was still quite young when the various schoolmasters received Wenker's questionnaires and that probably few, if any, had received any training in that discipline. The result was that Wenker received what amounted to 44,251 different phonetic transcriptions in 44,251 different phonetic alphabets. The problem of interpreting the data, of understanding which sounds were represented by the transcription of any one schoolmaster, was enormous, even though sound-to-spelling correspondences in German are much more regular than they are in English. Six maps based on the Wenker materials were published originally, and more have appeared since then, but the difficulties in interpreting the data remain.

Another problem arose as a result of Wenker's research: the dogma of the *Ausnahmslosigkeit der Lautgesetze* was not particularly supported by Wenker's findings. Wenker had assumed, and had hoped to demonstrate, that any particular phonetic change occurs in every word in which the relevant sound appears. On the contrary, Wenker showed, perhaps to his own dismay, that sound laws do indeed have exceptions. Put simply, we now know that, in the first stages, sound change may in fact be regular. After that, however, as the word spreads, every word has its own history. In other words, the Junggrammatiker were correct in their assessment of the nature of sound change, but only up to a point. Once a word begins to spread into other dialects, the regularity of the sound change breaks down.

Meanwhile, in France, at least one scholar had learned from the experiences of his German colleague. Jules Gilliéron began work in 1897 on what was to become the *Atlas linguistique de la France*. Unlike Wenker, Gilliéron employed a *fieldworker*, a man who went out into the various regions of France and collected phonetic data transcribed in a consistent phonetic alphabet. The fieldworker was a grocer by profession, one Edmond Edmont. That Edmont knew phonetics but had no knowledge of linguistics was regarded as an advantage by Gilliéron: the fieldworker would act as a kind of recording machine and would be uninfluenced by the vagaries of linguistic theory. He would just transcribe accurately the speech of his informants.

Edmont was also given the responsibility of choosing the specific communities in which he was to conduct his interviews for the French *Atlas*. In 500 of the 639 locations, Edmont interviewed only 1 informant; in the remaining 139 localities, he added material from auxiliary informants. In fact, in 2 localities he interviewed no fewer than 4 different people. Of the total number of 700 informants, only 60 were women, and the age of the informants ranged from fifteen to eight-five. Gilliéron also ranked the informants according to age and occupation, and approximately 200 of them were listed as well educated, "the local intellectuals." The remaining 500 had little significant formal education.

There were other differences between the French method and that of the Germans. Whereas Wenker sampled 40,736 localities with a brief questionnaire, Gilliéron sampled only 639 places in France, Belgium, Switzerland, and Italy with a questionnaire which included, depending upon its state of revision at the time, some 1,400 to 1,920 different items. On the other hand, it would be a mistake to say that the French and German atlases were totally different. In one important way they were the same: Wenker asked his schoolmasters to transcribe sentences from standard German into local dialect, and Edmont asked his informants direct questions in standard French. For example, Edmont asked, in French, of course, "How do you say *head*?"

We have no way of knowing exactly how the question technique affected the responses of the *Atlas* informants. We do know today that the ways in which questions are phrased can indeed prejudice informants' responses. Furthermore, the fact that Gilliéron used only one fieldworker meant that Edmont's weaknesses in phonetics, if any, are reflected in the *Atlas* itself. We know that all fieldworkers are weaker in some areas and stronger in others, and we know, further, that even superior fieldworkers have their bad days. We have no way to check the accuracy of Edmont's transcriptions, but as we shall see, such variations are a general problem with linguistic atlases created before the development of the portable tape recorder in the middle years of the twentieth century.

Gilliéron's influence was extraordinary and affected the history of dialect geography in important ways. Two of his students, Karl Jaberg and Jakob Jud, used many of their teacher's techniques in their own atlas of the dialects of Italy and the Italian-speaking part of Switzerland (*Sprach- und Sachatlas des Italiens und der Südschweiz*). Like all good students, Jaberg and Jud improved on the work of their teacher. They employed three questionnaires: a "normal," or basic, one containing about 2,000 items, used in 354 localities; a short form containing 800 items, used in 28 larger cities and towns; and a long form containing 4,000 items, used in 30 places to determine the vocabulary of larger sections of the area investigated. Lexical items predominated in all three versions of the questionnaire, but phonological and grammatical data were also elicited.

Jaberg and Jud sampled the Romansh and Italian language areas of Switzerland and all of Italy, Sicily, and Sardinia. Their three fieldworkers each took a different part of the area under study: (1) Switzerland and northern Italy, (2) southern Italy and Sicily, and (3) Sardinia. Furthermore, for the first time in dialect study, the method of asking the questions was indirect. Instead of asking, "How do you say *head*?" the fieldworkers elicited *head* by a gesture and a question: "What's this?" This technique was adopted and modified by both the American and the British dialectologists. In fact, Jud and Paul Scheuermeier, the main fieldworker for the Italian atlas, attended the training sessions in 1931 for the then fledgling *Linguistic Atlas of New England* (*LANE*), the first large-scale atlas-type research conducted on the English language.

## The Linguistic Atlas of New England

Although several studies had appeared before, we can take the year 1889 as marking the real beginning of serious dialect research in North America. In that year the American Dialect Society was founded, with its primary aim being the compilation of an American dialect dictionary on the model of Joseph Wright's *English Dialect Dictionary* (see below). Although that goal has not been accomplished to date, the Society provided a focal point for scholars, and some interesting research was carried out under the Society's auspices. On the other hand, the Society in those early days was not particularly aggressive in attracting membership, and during its first fifty years only six volumes of its journal, *Dialect Notes*, appeared. During this same period however, after the appearance of the German, French, and Italian atlases, scholars connected with the Society decided that a linguistic atlas would be more feasible and useful than a dictionary. It was also felt that an atlas would provide the relevant groundwork for later work on the dictionary itself. (*The Dictionary of American Regional English*, under the direction of Frederic G. Cassidy, will meet this goal upon its publication.)

The linguistic atlas project got under way in 1929. At its head was Hans Kurath, who even at that early stage of dialect research in North America had already written two articles on regional differences in American English. It is worth noting that in the first of the two articles Kurath had used the term *general American* to describe all American speech west of the Allegheny Mountains and north of the Ohio River. In the second article he rejected this notion and pointed out that there is no such thing as general American, that there is significant dialect variation everywhere in the United States. Strangely enough, as we saw in the last chapter, the notion still survives that there exists some mystical standard of pronunciation, devoid of regional association. The linguistic atlas, under Kurath's direction, was to prove conclusively that such a variety of American English simply does not exist.

After the atlas was founded, financial support was granted by the American Philosophical Society, the American Council of Learned Societies, and several American universities. The first task was to decide where to begin the research, and after considerable debate Kurath and his associates chose New England. Their reasons were both scholarly and pragmatic:

1. New England provided a compact area, so that travel from one place to another was not a major problem.
2. New England is probably unique in North America for its number of historical societies interested in the region's history and culture.
3. Information on New England speech in certain areas was already available, in large part because of the habits of the American academic community. Professors often did some research during their holidays, and *Dialect Notes* contained several studies of Cape Cod and Maine.
4. New England dialects are primary; the area is one of original English settlement. Areas such as Ohio, another locale suggested for the first atlas, are secondary, settled for the most part by people from the primary areas.
5. Many New England towns have full settlement histories recorded in town annals, so that in some cases it was possible to know from what areas in England the first settlers came.
6. Because of the compactness of the area, it was felt that results could be achieved relatively quickly and could thus provide the basis for proposals for additional funds for further research.

The fieldwork was planned for a two-year period. It was decided to sample every community of original settlement along the eastern seaboard and then sample more selectively farther west. In all, the *Linguistic Atlas of New England* interviewed informants in 416 communities.

In the *Handbook of the Linguistic Geography of New England* (Kurath et al. 1939), the authors outlined the instructions to fieldworkers regarding the selection of informants:

> 1. In every community selected for the study an elderly descendant of an old local family was to be included: a simple but intelligent farmer or farmer's wife in rural districts, a working man, tradesman, or shopkeeper in larger villages and cities. It was regarded as important to record this old-fashioned and most definitely local type in every community, in order that the earlier regional pattern might be accurately delineated and the oldest living forms of speech preserved as fully as possible for the historian of New England speech. Since most of the informants of this type are over 70 and not a few over 80, it would seem that we shall be able to establish the regionalism of the pre-industrial era of New England in considerable detail, with the possible exception of the highly urbanized area around Boston.
>
> 2. The second informant in each community was to be a middle-aged man or woman, native to the community, who had received better schooling (high school or academy in addition to grammar school), read more widely or enjoyed contacts with the better educated. This type is represented in about four-fifths of the communities. In others, more or less cultured informants were selected instead.
>
> 3. Cultured informants, with a college education or the equivalent, were to be chosen in most of the larger cities, including all the older cultural centers, and in a number of smaller communities. This type is represented in approximately one-fifth of the communities; three-fourths of these are in urbanized southern New England, one-fourth in the largely rural north. [p. 41]

The informants were thus categorized in the following manner:

Type I:    Little formal education, little reading, and restricted social contacts.

Type II:   Better formal education (usually high school) and/or wider reading and social contacts.

Type III:  Superior education (usually college), cultural background, wide reading and/or extensive social contacts.
                                                                                    [p. 44]

In addition to this classification of social types based on education, the *LANE* had a further classification of informants based on their age:

Type A: Aged and/or regarded by the fieldworker as old-fashioned.

Type B: Middle-aged or younger, and/or regarded by the fieldworker as more modern.

[p. 44]

All informants, regardless of type, were required to be natives of their areas and to have lived there all their lives, with no significant travel to other locales. An ideal type I-A informant, then, would be a seventy-five-year-old illiterate farmer who is a member of the oldest living generation of the area in which he lives. Because the *LANE* interviewed type II informants as well, and did so in some 80 percent of the localities, the Americans can be credited with the first linguistic atlas study of what Kurath called the "common speech." All preceding atlases concentrated essentially on "folk speech," the speech of *LANE* I-A informants. It is also important to bear in mind that the type II informants in 1930 had attended high school, if they were aged seventy or so, in the 1870s and 1880s. Many had received a good education in Latin and some even in Greek, and of course such people were far more highly educated than today's graduate of even the best high school. Type III informants, college educated, were certainly rarer in 1930 than they are today.

The fieldworkers for the *LANE* were themselves all experienced linguists and phoneticians, but Kurath felt that some effort should be made to limit, as much as possible, individual differences in the fieldworkers' phonetic transcriptions. Hence training sessions were held. All field records were transcribed in a finely graded phonetic alphabet. Raven I. McDavid, Jr., explains:

> It is obvious, of course, that there will be differences between field-workers in the way they handle such a finely graded phonetic system as the alphabet for the American Atlas. Differences are greater, of course, when the field-workers have no training in common; much less if they have worked closely together over a period of time. There is, in fact, a remarkable degree of correlation between the transcriptions of field-workers who have had the same kind of training. Consequently, one may feel considerable confidence in the transcriptions of any experienced field-worker, at least so far as the vowels and consonants are concerned. [McDavid 1958:493]

In preparing the questionnaire, or *worksheets*, as the Americans called them, Kurath and his colleagues consulted numerous sources, the most important of which were the already published studies in *Dialect Notes*, the journal *American Speech*, and Alexander Ellis's *dialect test* (see below).

The major criterion for the inclusion of a term in the worksheets was the existence of regional variants. For example, there are several terms in North America for the earthworm: *angleworm, angledog, eaceworm, mud-worm, fish(ing) worm, earthworm*. Also, the terms had to be familiar to the prospective informants, and, very important, the terms had to be relatively easy to elicit during a fairly relaxed conversation. That is, the worksheets were intended to be used by fieldworkers as only a base; the fieldworker was responsible for eliciting the specific terms in a free conversation, for only in this way could they be more or less certain that the informants were using as natural a language as possible, given the interview situation: the aim was to call forth the language that one uses, perhaps, with a friendly stranger. This "conversational technique" was a significant change in the methods of atlas interviewing, since for the first time there was no set way to ask the questions. It was left to the fieldworkers to elicit the specific items on the worksheets in ways which worked best for them.

The worksheets for the *LANE* contained slightly more than 700 items. They were first field tested, then revised, and only then put into use in actual fieldwork for the *Atlas of New England*. The worksheets elicited three different types of data. We noted above an example of a lexical item: the different terms for *earthworm*. The *Atlas* also sought to elicit phonological data, such as whether *mourning* and *morning* or *merry, Mary*, and *marry* are homophonous. The third type of data is essentially grammatical in nature and is the main reason why the American fieldworkers tried to elicit forms in as relaxed an atmosphere as possible. The stress here was on forms of the verb, such as variants for the past tense: *sot* for *sat* or *hain't* for *haven't*.

The fieldwork for the *LANE* was completed in 1933, and then began the long process of editing the field records for publication. Kurath decided to follow the lead of Wenker and Gilliéron and to reproduce the actual transcriptions on maps. Each item of the worksheets was to have its own separate map. In addition to the maps themselves, he also presented a commentary on the overleaf of each map. The commentaries contain information such as (1) positive or negative attitudes toward a particular word, (2) whether the word was regarded by certain informants as old-fashioned, (3) deviant meanings, and so on.

In 1939, Kurath and his associates published the *Handbook of the Linguistic Geography of New England*. In addition to providing a detailed description of the methods employed, the *Handbook* gives a full settlement history of the region, brief biographies of all the informants, and some major conclusions about the dialect areas of New England. The major dialect boundary runs northward from the mouth of the Connecticut River through the states of Connecticut and Massachusetts to

Franklin County, Massachusetts. The line then turns westward to the Berkshire Mountains and then northward again to the crest of the Green Mountains and the northern boundary of the state of Vermont, hence dividing New England into two major dialect areas: east and west.

These two areas are delineated mainly in terms of phonology and lexicon. The most notable difference is the pronunciation of /r/ in post-vocalic position, as in *car* or *barn*. In western New England, the pronunciation is what people generally regard as typically "American," with the /r/ fully pronounced (*constricted* is the correct phonetic description), whereas in eastern New England the pronunciation of these words is quite similar to *RP*. The vocabulary differences are many. The most striking include *stone drag*, *white bread*, and *funnel* in the east, as compared with *stone boat*, *wheat bread*, and *stove pipe*, respectively, in the west.

Kurath was also able to make some sociolinguistic comments on the data. Certain grammatical forms appeared only in the speech of the older, less educated informants (type I-A). For example, only the older, less educated generation in northeastern New England uses *riz* for *rose* or *has risen* (in "the sun rose" and "the sun has risen") or *div* or *dived* or *dove* (in "he dived/dove into the water"). Because there has been compulsory education in many parts of New England since colonial times, it is not surprising to find many innovations in the local speech. Newer terms from the cities are replacing the older folk terminology. *Earthworm* is replacing local terms such as *angledog*, *eaceworm*, *fishworm*, or *mudworm*; *seesaw* is replacing *teetertotter*, *tinter*, *dandle*, *teedle*, or *tilter*; *pantry* is replacing *buttery*; *clothes closet* is replacing *clothes press*; *at home* is replacing *to home* (in "he is ——— home"). There are also innovations in pronunciation, one of them being the articulation of *boil* with the vowel of *oil* in place of the (older) vowel of *high*.

On the other hand, many relics remain. On the seaboard, informants from mainly rural areas use *fairing up* (*off*, *away*) for *clearing up* (in "the weather is . . ."); and in rural Maine the common term for a *knoll* is a *rubble*. These, as well as the grammatical items mentioned earlier (*riz*, *div*, and so forth), are, not surprisingly, found in the speech of the older and less educated informants.

Using the *LANE* data, coupled with data gleaned from later fieldwork, Kurath was able to state quite positively that only western New England speech has had much influence on the speech of areas farther inland. He stated, further, that one of the *LANE*'s main goals was to stimulate additional research on the dialects of North American English, both in New England and in other areas as well. The *LANE* was never intended to exhaust the possibilities for additional study. As McDavid writes: "A linguistic atlas does not and cannot attempt to answer all the questions about dialect differences, but . . . its principal purpose is to provide a

framework of territorial distribution and historical perspective within
which further questions may be asked most intelligently." (McDavid
1958:491)

We noted in chapter 1 that the test for all dialectology is that of
objectivity; in *LANE*, this test is certainly met. For example, the *Handbook*
lists brief biographies for each informant, and thus the reader can judge
if the informants were correctly typed in terms of education and age.
Furthermore, after the field records were edited, each fieldworker was
ranked in comparison with his or her coworkers in terms of phonetic
accuracy, ability to elicit conversational forms, and skill in eliciting nonstandard grammatical forms. By using these data, scholars today can also
evaluate the information provided on the maps. Nearly half a century
has passed since the completion of the *LANE* fieldwork, and during that
time much of the United States and Canada has also been studied. In the
next section, we shall examine this research and, equally important, that
based on the fieldwork for these atlases.

## Studies Based on Linguistic Atlas Field Records

In the decades which have passed since the publication of the *LANE*,
most of the fieldwork for the rest of North America has been initiated,
and the work for the eastern part of the United States has been completed. The *Linguistic Atlas of the Upper Midwest (LAUM)*, under the edi-
torship of Harold Allen, appeared in 1973–1977 (see below) and the
*Linguistic Atlas of the Middle and South Atlantic States*, edited by Raven I.
McDavid, Jr., is in the process of publication. Lee Pederson's *Linguistic
Atlas of the Gulf States* is also now nearing completion. Work is still under-
way on the *Linguistic Atlas of the Pacific Northwest*, under the direction of
Carroll Read and Allan Metcalf. The *Linguistic Atlas of Oklahoma* and the
*Linguistic Atlas of the North-Central States* were taken over by McDavid
after the death of their first editors, William R. Van Riper and Albert H.
Marckwardt, respectively. In addition to these atlases themselves, a significant amount of research based on the analysis of atlas records has
been published. Since this work has permitted us to draw dialect boundaries for much of the eastern United States, we shall examine some of it
briefly. Figure 2–1, for example, shows the approximate location of all
the communities which have been surveyed by atlas fieldworkers in the
far eastern United States, excluding Georgia, Florida, and northern
New England.

In 1949, Hans Kurath published the first major study based on atlas
work: *A Word Geography of the Eastern United States*. By then it was already
clear that the old distinction between northern, southern, and general

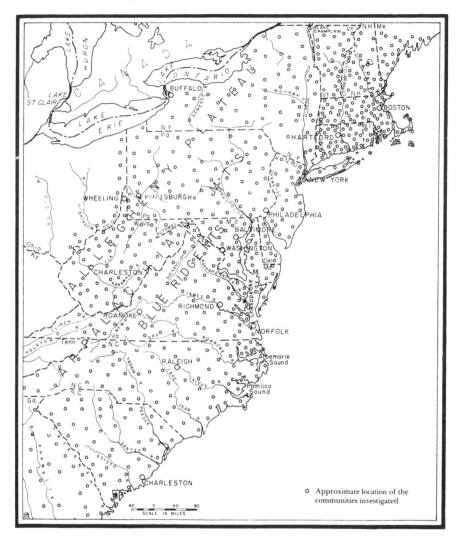

*Figure 2–1.* Area of the Atlas Survey. *Source*: Atwood 1953: figure 1.

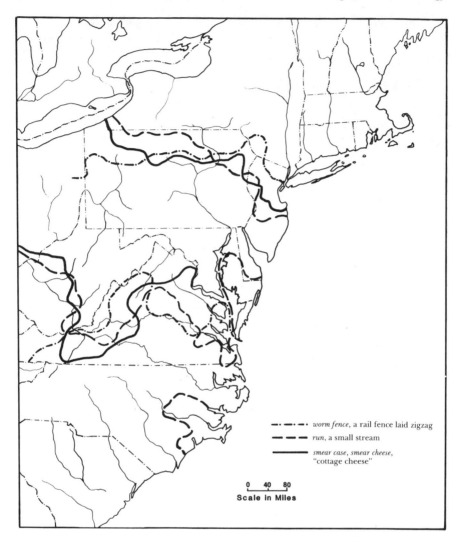

*Figure 2–2.* Three Isoglosses of the North Midland. *Source*: Kurath 1949: figure 18.

American was not productive; in fact, Kurath's work indicated a large dialect area between the North and the South: the *Midland*. As the title of Kurath's study indicates, he examined all the lexical material from the worksheets and was able to draw *isoglosses* showing the various usages transcribed by the fieldworkers. Figure 2–2 shows three such isoglosses, which help to delineate the North Midland dialect area. Since an isogloss is a line drawn on a map to isolate different elements of pronunciation, grammar, or vocabulary, a *bundle of isoglosses* can indicate a dialect boundary. The South can be set off from the South Midland area by several words. The bundle of isoglosses in figure 2–3, for *low* (the sound a cow makes), *lightwood* (small, light pieces of wood used to start a fire), and a call to cows to bring them home from the field provides one of Kurath's examples.

Kurath's study provided a powerful testimony to the variety which exists in American English. A small stream of fresh water was a *brook* in the North, a *run* in the Midland, and a *branch* in the South. The *best man* at a wedding was known as the *waiter* in parts of the South. The outside toilet was an *outhouse* in the North (except New England), a *water closet* in New England and Philadelphia, a *closet* in the Ohio valley, a *garden house* in Virginia and northeastern North Carolina, a *johnny, johnny house*, or *jack house* in other parts of Virginia and, perhaps the best of all, a *necessary* in Boston and parts of the Deep South. *Merry Christmas*, the common Christmas greeting in most of the United States, was *Christmas Gift* in parts of the South and South Midland. These and dozens of other examples eliminated forever, at least as far as serious scholarship was concerned, the myth of the general American dialect, and in its place came the three major (and numerous minor) dialect areas which, by lexical evidence alone, were delineated by the *Word Geography*, Kurath's pioneering study.

In 1953, E. Bagby Atwood published the second major study which was based on atlas data: *A Survey of Verb Forms in the Eastern United States*. Atwood analyzed the grammatical evidence in the worksheets and thus was able to draw fairly clear dialect boundaries based on these data. Figure 2–4 shows the distribution of the past tense of *dive*, and figure 2–5 maps the various forms of the past tense of *drink*. In the latter case, occurrences of *drank* are not mapped; only the nonstandard forms are listed. In all, Atwood published some thirty-one maps with commentary. He pointed out which forms were used only by type I informants and which were more widespread, which forms were used mainly by black informants, which forms were exclusively northern, southern, or midland, and so on. On his last two maps, Atwood draws isoglosses which illustrate the extent to which verb forms have spread. Figure 2–6, for

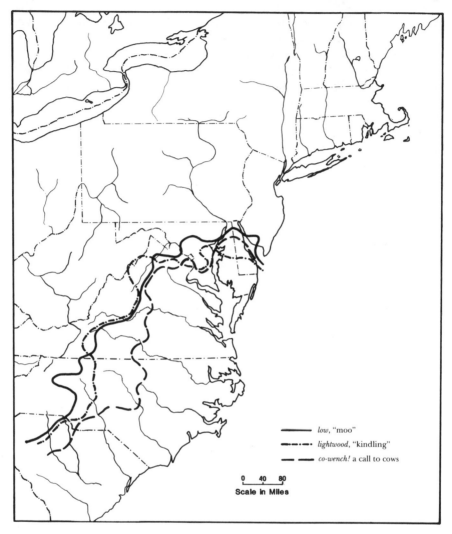

*Figure 2–3.* Three Isoglosses of the South. *Source*: Kurath 1949: figure 29.

example, shows his isoglosses for *might could (could)*, *I holp (helped) myself*, and *he mought (might) have*.

Once again, as with Kurath's study, atlas records were the best possible evidence for the wide variety in American English, in both its standard and nonstandard forms. Atwood was able to show, for example, that standard English is in no way monolithic; on the contrary, Atwood's evidence demonstrates that a verb such as *might could* (in "he might could do that"), while nonstandard in the North, is very much standard in the South. Type III informants use the expression all the time, at least in speech, if not in writing. The fact that such a verb form is not found in grammar books in no way makes it less standard, given our definition of the term.

The attempt to characterize the speech of type III informants, the speakers of standard dialects, was carried still further by Kurath and McDavid (1961) in their *Pronunciation of English in the Atlantic States (PEAS)*. As the title of their study indicates, Kurath and McDavid analyzed the phonological data from the worksheets. The overwhelming stress here is on the vowels; there is little analysis of the consonants. The results of their analysis were (1) that they were able to draw dialect boundaries for the area under consideration and (2) that they were able to demonstrate the wide variety of pronunciations which exist under the general rubric of standard American English. For example, the pronunciation of a type III informant from Philadelphia, Pennsylvania, differs greatly from that of a counterpart in Williamsburg, Virginia, or Hartford, Connecticut, yet by every criterion which we can use, all three speak the standard English dialect of their particular regions.

Furthermore, we can check Kurath's and McDavid's conclusions as to the nature of standard English because, in the best tradition of scholarship, they provide us with (1) short biographies of the type III informants included in their study and (2) the actual phonetic transcriptions from the field records. The authors also analyze the data into phonemes and include the allophones of the phonemes in some eighty charts which list the vowels used by each of the type III informants.

By 1961, scholars were able to draw fairly distinct dialect boundaries for the eastern United States, excluding the Gulf states and the Deep South. Figure 2–7 shows the major and minor dialect areas drawn by Kurath and McDavid, and the picture they drew has not changed significantly. It is worth noting here that these boundaries drawn from phonological data are supported and corroborated by both lexical and grammatical evidence. Each of the three kinds of data from the worksheets tends to reinforce the others, the result being that we have a reasonably clear picture of the dialect areas of New England and the Middle and South Atlantic states.

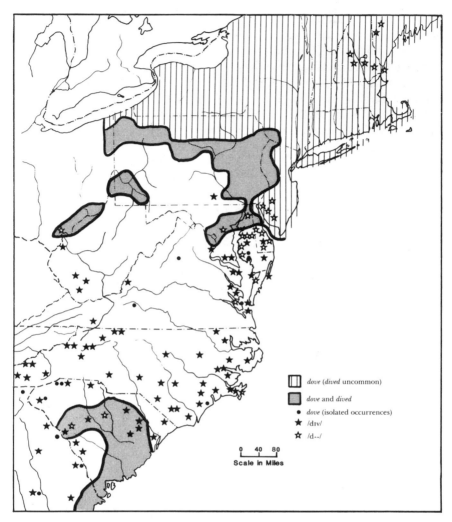

*Figure 2–4.* Distribution of *Dived* (Preterite). *Source*: Atwood
1953: figure 6.

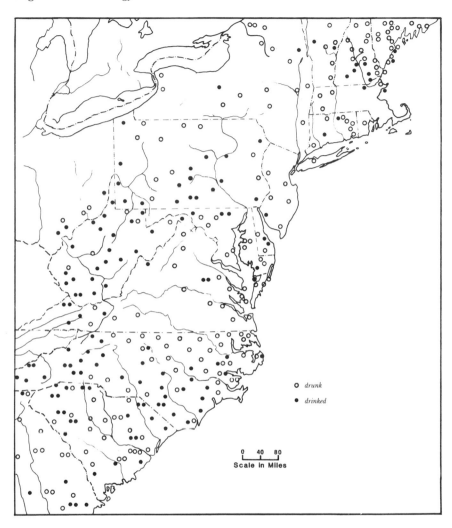

*Figure 2–5.* Distribution of *Drank* (Preterite). *Source*: Atwood 1953: figure 7.

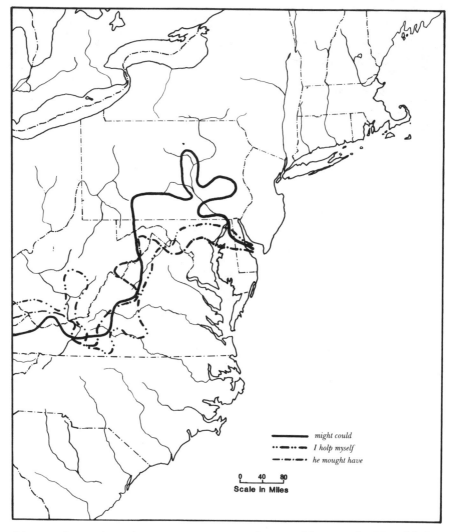

*Figure 2–6.* Southern Forms: *Might Could, I Holp Myself, He Mought Have. Source*: Atwood 1953: figure 31.

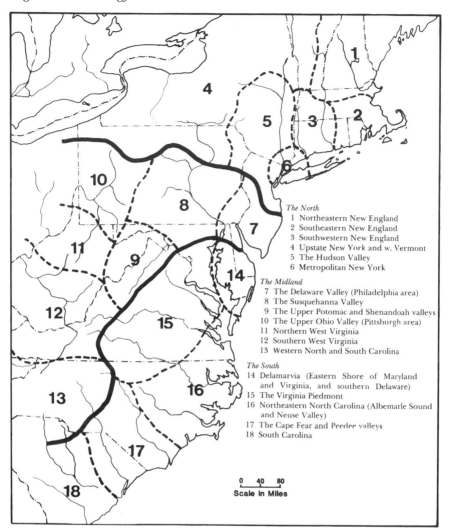

The North
1 Northeastern New England
2 Southeastern New England
3 Southwestern New England
4 Upstate New York and w. Vermont
5 The Hudson Valley
6 Metropolitan New York

The Midland
7 The Delaware Valley (Philadelphia area)
8 The Susquehanna Valley
9 The Upper Potomac and Shenandoah valleys
10 The Upper Ohio Valley (Pittsburgh area)
11 Northern West Virginia
12 Southern West Virginia
13 Western North and South Carolina

The South
14 Delamarvia (Eastern Shore of Maryland and Virginia, and southern Delaware)
15 The Virginia Piedmont
16 Northeastern North Carolina (Albemarle Sound and Neuse Valley)
17 The Cape Fear and Peedee valleys
18 South Carolina

0 40 80
Scale in Miles

*Figure 2–7.* The Speech Areas of the Atlantic States. *Source:* Kurath and McDavid 1961: map 2.

The works of Kurath, Atwood, and Kurath and McDavid are the three major studies based on atlas field records for the East; each analyzed one of the three kinds of data elicited by the worksheets. In addition to these studies, however, there have been a large number of works on particular problems, and it is worthwhile to take a brief look at two of them before turning to the only published atlas since the *LANE*: Harold Allen's *Linguistic Atlas of the Upper Midwest*.

One of the best known of the more specific studies is Atwood's "Grease and Greasy: A Study of Geographical Variation" (1950). Atwood noted that even the most amateur observers of American speech have pointed out that some Americans say *greaze* and *greazy*, while others say *greasse* and *greassy*. By using data available at the time, Atwood was able to draw the map in figure 2–8. The northern limit of *greazy*, as the map indicates, runs more or less along the same line which delimits the North from the Midland. Atwood also notes that the common dictionary distinction, that *greassy* means "covered with grease" and that *greazy* is less literal and more pejorative in its connotations, has no basis in fact. South of what is now called *the greazy-greassy line*, *greazy* definitely means "covered with grease." Since the fieldworkers did not ask informants for any meaning differentiation, however, the atlas records do not provide any clues as to whether people in the North do indeed distinguish between the two pronunciations. Informants were asked to pronounce these words in contexts such as "When an axle squeaks, you . . . it" and "When you get it on your hands, they feel . . ."

By the middle years of the 1950s, much of the fieldwork for the various linguistic atlas projects had been completed. Albert H. Marckwardt, then director of the *Linguistic Atlas of the North-Central States*, analyzed the data from those field records to extend our knowledge of what happens to the isoglosses west of Pennsylvania, the western border of the three major studies of Atwood, Kurath, and Kurath and McDavid. Marckwardt used all three kinds of atlas data—phonological, lexical, and grammatical—and found that the relatively clearcut dialect patterns along the eastern seaboard became far more complex in the northern Midwest. Figures 2–9 and 2–10 demonstrate that the Midland boundary is fairly well defined in Ohio, Indiana, and Illinois but that west of the Mississippi River matters are not so simple. Marckwardt concluded his paper "Principal and Subsidiary Dialect Areas in the North-Central States" with the following statement: "At this point it is clear that we are dealing with a challenging and highly complex dialect situation: one which will require our drawing upon every available facet of cultural and settlement history to give it meaning and to make it understandable" (Marckwardt 1957:15). That situation has not changed considerably since Marckwardt's description of it. The complete *Linguis-*

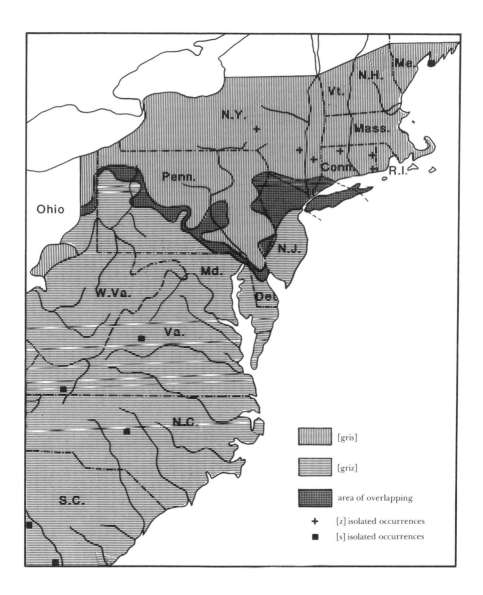

*Figure 2–8.* Distribution of *Greasse* and *Greaze. Source*: Atwood 1950.

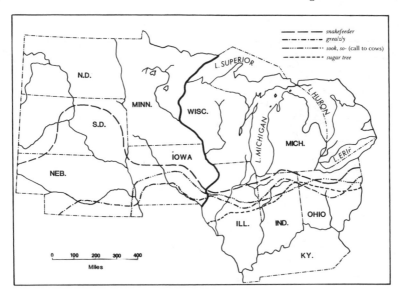

*Figure 2–9.* Isoglosses of the Upper Midwest: *Snakefeeder, Grea/z/y, Sook, So-, Sugar Tree. Source*: Marckwardt 1957.

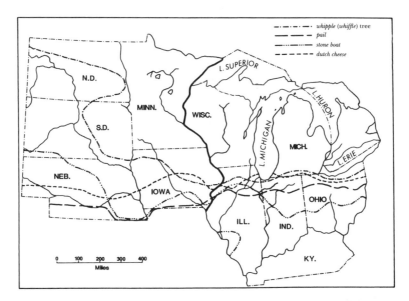

*Figure 2–10.* Isoglosses of the Upper Midwest: *Whipple (Whiffle) Tree, Pail, Stone Boat, Dutch Cheese. Source*: Marckwardt 1957.

*tic Atlas of the North-Central States,* with its additional data, will give us a clearer understanding of the dialect patterns in that part of the United States. Certainly the situation in the upper Midwest has been clarified to a great degree with the publication of that atlas, the first since the *LANE*.

## The Linguistic Atlas of the Upper Midwest

We saw earlier that the *LANE* was published more or less according to schedule between 1939 and 1943 and that since then most of the fieldwork for other atlases has been completed. It took thirty years, however, for another linguistic atlas to appear: *The Linguistic Atlas of the Upper Midwest* (*LAUM*), under the directorship of Harold Allen. The *LAUM* used essentially the same techniques as did the *LANE* insofar as field procedures are concerned, and it has the familiar three informant types. There are, however, significant differences between the two studies.

The first and most obvious difference concerns the format of the *LAUM*. Whereas the *LANE* was published in large folio volumes which contained maps of the area with the fieldworkers' actual transcriptions, the *LAUM* presents the data in a different manner. Both the lexical information and the grammatical material are presented in ways such as those shown in figure 2–11. Some small maps are included, but the data are mainly presented in the form of lists of informant responses, called *list manuscripts*. In the case of *blow*, we see that Allen gives a general discussion of the findings, often linking his results to earlier studies. Then comes the list of the responses of each informant. With *boil*, no map is presented, but we do find a brief discussion followed by the list manuscript.

The phonological data for the *LAUM* are presented differently. Following the model of Kurath's and McDavid's *Pronunciation of English in the Atlantic States,* Allen presents the transcriptions of the stressed vowels in grids such as that in figure 2–12. As we see, the data have been analyzed into phonemes of sorts, and the transcriptions have been transferred to the grids.

Another important way in which the *LAUM* differs from the *LANE* is that whereas the *LANE* presents phonetic transcriptions only, the *LAUM* gives the reader both regional and sociolinguistic analyses. In the case of *are not* in figure 2–13, in addition to the general discussion of the item, we also find percentages of responses, both in terms of the three types of informants and in terms of the five states included in the *LAUM* survey: Minnesota, Iowa, North Dakota, South Dakota, and Nebraska.

We shall return to the problem of using percentages in chapter 3, but

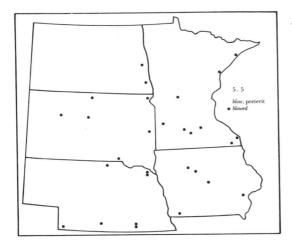

5.5

*blow*, preterit
• *blowed*

*blow*

5.5 The wind *blew* hard. NE 637, VF 6, 38, 42.

Historical *blew* predominates in the UM as the preterit of *blow*. Analogical *blowed* is found in the speech of four out of five Type I infs. but in the speech of less than one-tenth of the Type II's. *Blowed* apparently is declining, since its incidence is much higher in most of the eastern states. Atwood found it in the speech of more than one-half of the Type I infs. in northern New England and of more than nine-tenths of those in North Carolina, although it is unusual in western New England, eastern New York, and eastern Pennsylvania.

No sharp Northern-Midland contrast is evident in the UM, where Minnesota's 14% frequency of *blowed* is only slightly higher than that in Iowa. But the decline of *blowed* is apparent even within the UM, since it is rare in the more recently settled regions of Minnesota and in the western third of the Dakotas and Nebraska. Like several others, this form seems to have suffered from attacks in the schools.

Inf. 220 also has *blowed* as participle.

blew 1–5, 7–15, 17–26, 28–34, 36–43, 45–50, 52–55, 57–60, 62–65; 101–13, 115–17, 119–31, cr?132, 133–37, 139–50, 152; 201–9, !210, 211–19, 221–26; 301, 304–6, 308–16, 318–21, 323–28; 401–2, c403, 404, 406, 408–25, 427–29, 431, 433–37.

blowed c6, 16, 27, c35, c42, 44, c51, 56, cvr64; c113, 114, 132, 138, 142; 220, c225; 302–3, 307, c314, 317, c322; c405, 407, c408, c429, 430, 432, c433.

no response 61; 118, 151; 426.

Comment:
*blowed*: Corrected to 'blew' but inf. consistently uses 'blowed' in conversation.—132.

*boil*

37.2 *boiled* eggs. NE 294. VF 6.

In the UM *boiled* is the overwhelming choice as the participial adjective of *boil*. Three scattered instances of *boilt* appear in the speech of Type I infs. in northern Minnesota, northern North Dakota, and southern Nebraska. Statistically insignificant, these three nevertheless echo the conclusion of Atwood that *boilt* is distinctly a Type I usage in areas where the form itself is in the minority, Atwood's VF reports *boilt* as limited largely to the Midland speech area, but with a sprinkling of occurrences throughout the Middle and South Atlantic states excepting South Carolina and Georgia.

boiled /bɔild/ c1, 2–5, c6, 7–15, 17–22, !23, 24–50, c51–52, 53–58, c59, 60–61, c62, 63–65; 101–22, 124–41, 143, 146–50, 152; 201–5, 207–26; 301–4, 306–10, 312–26, c327, 328; 401–28, 430–37.

boilt /bɔilt/ 16; 206; 429.

no response 23; 142, 144–45, 151; 305, 311.

*Figure 2–11. LAUM: Blow and Boil. Source: Allen 1973:9.*

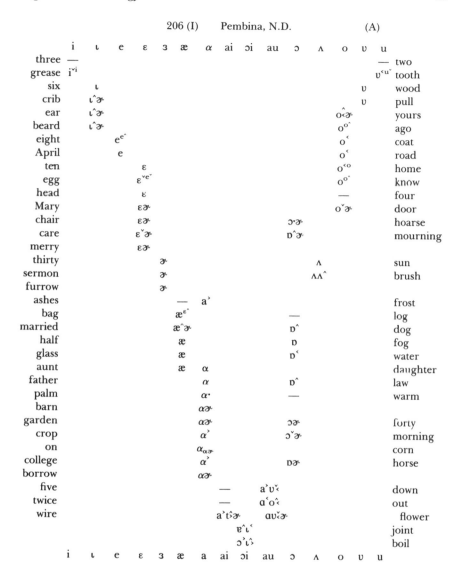

*Figure 2–12. LAUM*: Transcriptions of Stressed Vowels in Pembina, North Dakota. *Source*: Allen 1976:161.

*are not*

21.2c They *are not* going to hurt him. NE 674.

The third-person present plural negative of *be* appears in the indicated or a similar context. Four expressions occur: *They ain't, they are not, they're not*, and *they aren't*. The last three are tabulated together as instances of *are*.

The incidence of *ain't* here is lower than with the first- and third-person singular constructions, but its frequency is consistently higher among the less-educated infs. One Minnesota farmer, a Type III inf., uses it freely. One instance of South Midland *hain't* is included from the speech of a Type I Iowan of Kentucky and Tennessee parentage.

The variations with *are* dominate in all states of the UM and among all three groups.

|         | Type I | Type II | Type III |
|---------|--------|---------|----------|
| *ain't* | 38%    | 17%     | 10%      |
| *are not*, |      |         |          |
| etc.    | 66%    | 83%     | 90%      |

|         | Mn. | Ia. | N.D. | S.D. | Nb. | Ave. |
|---------|-----|-----|------|------|-----|------|
| *ain't* | 24% | 27% | 40%  | 40%  | 17% | 26%  |
| *are not*, |  |     |      |      |     |      |
| etc.    | 80% | 70% | 80%  | 60%  | 87% | 75%  |

they ain't /ðe ent/ c15, c19, c27, c43, 50, c51–52, c56–57, c59; c105, c107, 121, c124, sn127, *134, 142–43, 147; 207, c220, c225; 302–3, 311, c314, 317, 320, c322; c401, 405, 430, 432, c436. they hain't /ðe hent/ c135.

they are not /ðe ɑr nɑt/ 21, 49; ?145. they're not /ðɛr nɑt/ 1–5, 10, 20, 23–24, 28, 32–34, c40, 41, c52, 54–55, 58, c59, 64–65; c102, 103, 109–10, 112–14, c117, 120–21, 133, 137–40; 207, 214, 221; 304, 309, c321, 324, 326, 328; 402–3, 408, 413–14, 416, 420–21, 423–24, 427, 431, 437.

they aren't /ðe ɑrnt/ 7, 14, 26, c43, c47, c53, c61–63; c102, 106, 111, 122–23, 126, ?128, 130–31, 136, 146, 149, f150; 218; 310, 312–13; 401, 406, 410–12, 422.

no response 8–9, 11–13, 16–18, 22, 25, 29–31, 35–39, 42, 44–46, 48, 60; 101, 104, 108, 115–16, 118–19, 125, 129, 132, 141, 144, 148, 151–52; 201–5, 208–13, 215–17, 219–20, 222–23, 224, 226; 301, 305–8, 315–19, 323, 325, 327; 404, 407, 409, 415, 417–19, 425–26, 428–29, 433–35.

Comment:

*ain't*: Inf.'s wife gets after him if he uses 'ain't'—122. "I try not to say it because it don't sound good"—127. Inf. has carefully taught himself to avoid 'ain't'—312. "I try not to say 'ain't,' but do sometimes without thinking"—424.

*Figure 2–13. LAUM*: Analysis of *Are Not. Source*: Allen 1975:39.

for now it is worth noting that the *LAUM*'s use of percentages creates quite a few problems for the reader. For example, figure 2–13 indicates that some 10 percent of the type III informants use *ain't* for *are not*, but of the 208 informants of the *LAUM* survey, only 16 are classified as type III. How *could* 1.6 persons (10 percent) have used *ain't*? Moreover, since only two type III informants used *ain't*, we can question the relevance of percentages for such small numbers.

Another difference between the *LAUM* and the *LANE* concerns the classification of informants into types. Whereas the *LANE* categorized informants as to both education and age, using I, II, or III for the former and A or B for the latter, the *LAUM*'s system is simpler. Type I informants are like the *LANE*'s type I-A—older, with little formal education. *LAUM*'s type II is the *LANE*'s II-B—middle-aged, with a secondary school education. *LAUM*'s type III is the *LANE*'s III-B—middle-aged with a college education. In other words, the *LAUM*'s type II and type III informants are not differentiated according to age. Type I informants, on the other hand, are considerably older than the other two types. As we shall see later in this chapter, the *LANE* came under considerable attack for its informant types, yet the *LAUM* has even fewer classifications than does the *LANE*, published thirty years before.

In spite of all these problems, however, the *LAUM* must be considered an important contribution to the study of American linguistic geography. All the data are presented in list manuscripts, and even if the use of percentages in certain places is questionable, the reader can always go to the lists to discover the linguistic patterns evidenced by the *LAUM* informants for any particular item of the worksheets. And since all linguistic atlases are intended to be research tools, the *LAUM* meets that requirement more than adequately.

The *LAUM* was not only the first linguistic atlas to be published since the *LANE* but also the last so far, although, as we noted earlier, the *Linguistic Atlas of the Middle and South Atlantic States* is at this writing in its early stages of publication. Here, it seems, is a good place to leave North America and turn to the other major study of English dialects: Harold Orton's *Survey of English Dialects* (*SED*).

## *Survey of English Dialects*: **Background**

There have been comments on the wide dialectal variety in Britain from very early times. In 1387, Edward Trevisa published his translation of Higden's *Polychronicon* (*Polychronicon Ranulphi Higden Monachi Cestrensis*) and noted: "Al þe longage of þe Norþhumbres, and specialliche at ʒork, is so scharp, slitting, and frotynge, and vnschape, þat we souþerne

men may þat longage unneþe vnderstonde" (quoted in Wakelin
1972:34). In his preface to *Eneydos*, one hundred years after Trevisa,
William Caxton wrote extensively on the difference in English dialects in
his day. The following (quoted in Wakelin 1972) is especially interesting:

> And certaynly our language now vsed varyeth ferre from that whiche was
> vsed and spoken when I was borne / For we englysshe men / ben borne
> vnder the domynacyon of the mone, whiche is neuer stedfaste / but euer
> wauering / wexynge one season / and waneth & dyscreaseth another
> season / And that comyn englysshe that is spoken on one shyre varyeth
> from a nother. In so moche that in my dayes happened that certayne
> marchauntes were in a shippe in taymse, for to haue sayled ouer the see
> into zeland / and for lacke of wynde, thei taryed atte forlond, and wente
> to lande for to refreshe them; And one of theym named sheffelde, a
> mercer, cam in-to an hows and axed for mete; and specyally he axyd after
> eggys; And the goode wyf answerde, that she could speke no frenshe. And
> the merchaunt was angry, for he also coude speke no frenshe, but wolde
> haue hadde egges / and she vnderstode hym not / And thenne at laste a
> nother sayd that he wolde haue eyren / then the good wyf sayd that she
> vnderstod hym well / Loo, what sholde a man in thyse dayes now wryte,
> egges or eyren / certaynly it is harde to playse euery man / by cause of
> dyuersite & chaunge of language. [p. 35]

Many people have commented on the variety of English speech, and it
is not surprising that scholars began turning their attention to this subject. In fact, the early English lexicographers of the seventeenth century
included a few dialect words in their books. (See, for example, Elisha
Cole's *English Dictionary* [1656] and Stephen Skinner's *Etymologicon Lin-
guae Anglicanae* [1671].) Even before these early dictionaries, there
appeared Dean Laurence Nowell's *Vocabularium Saxonicum*, written
probably around 1565. Nowell included numerous dialect words from
his time which, in his opinion, were survivals from the Old English
period but were no longer used in the English of London. Nowell himself was from Lancashire, and of the approximately 200 dialect entries in
the *Vocabularium Saxonicum* all but 17 are from this county, thus providing a valuable contribution to our knowledge of the Lancashire dialect of
Nowell's time. The following is one of his entries: "Haȝan. Hawes. The
frute of the white thorne or howthorne. Lanc., hagges" (quoted in
Wakelin 1972:44).

The earliest interest in dialect in England paralleled a general interest
in slang, cant, and argot. In fact, by the end of the sixteenth century,
several books had already appeared on the subject of the language of
English criminals. The first more or less scholarly treatment of the sub-

ject was *A New Dictionary of the Terms Ancient and Modern of the Canting Crew, in its Several Tribes of Gipsies, Beggars, Thieves, Cheats, Etc.* The author of this important work, however, has never been identified; he published the work over the initials B.E. and dealt only cursorily with dialects as we have been using the term.

In 1785, nearly a century after B.E.'s work, came the first edition of Captain Francis Grose's *Classical Dictionary of the Vulgar Tongue.* The book was advertised as a list of cant terms used by criminals, but it also contained a significant number of words which in Grose's day were regionally distributed in England. In addition to his research on the language of the denizens of London by night, Grose made several forays into the countryside to collect dialect material. On one of these field trips, Grose met Robert Burns and hence became the first (and in all probability the last) English lexicographer-dialectologist to find his way into the works of a major poet. In fact, Burns wrote two poems about Grose, the best known of which, "On the Late Captain Grose's Peregrinations thro' Scotland," contains the couplet: "Now, by the Powers o' Verse and Prose! / Thou art a dainty chield, O Grose!—" Although Grose did borrow heavily from B.E. at times, he also added much new material and, at the same time, eliminated some of the more dubious entries made by B.E. Grose's first edition of 1785 contained approximately 3,000 entries. His later work, the *Provincial Glossary with a Collection of Local Proverbs, and Popular Superstitions,* appeared in 1787 and contained much new dialect material.

The first major study of dialect pronunciation in England was Alexander J. Ellis's *On Early English Pronunciation* (1869–1889). One of the more interesting aspects of Ellis's study is his dialect test. He made a list of some 970 words which he asked his informants, mainly members of the clergy, to pronounce. Ellis then transcribed the responses in what amounted to a phonetic alphabet of his own creation (the International Phonetic Alphabet had not yet been developed). Ellis drew ten dialect boundaries which, he said, marked the major dialect areas of England, Scotland, and Wales; unfortunately, his conclusions must remain a trifle suspect, since he did little transcribing in the field. Rather, he reconstructed his informants' speech at a later time, after he had finished the interviews. His study nonetheless provides excellent source material and many texts and poems in local dialects.

The most important work on English dialects in what we are calling here the early stages of dialect research in Britain is Joseph Wright's six-volume work, *English Dialect Dictionary.* Wright himself demonstrated that, in the England of the nineteenth century, one could indeed rise from humble beginnings. He learned to write only as an adult, at Leeds, and later received advanced degrees in Germany. At the time he began work on his *Dictionary*, he was deputy professor of comparative philology at Oxford.

Much of Wright's material for the *English Dialect Dictionary* came from the files of the English Dialect Society, then recently founded (1873), which had already underwritten dialect research in many of the counties. In addition to these studies, however, Wright also collected a considerable amount of additional data, mostly from volunteers. His objective, he said, was to compile a record of all the dialect words in English, and here he meant British English different from the London standard. In spite of this impressive goal, Wright's results, by modern standards at least, were quite uneven. The dialects of Wright's native Yorkshire receive the most complete coverage; the rest of the country is covered only in a rather general fashion. Furthermore, Wright's collection contains a large number of unusual words, but many of the common ones, such as the numerous synonyms for *earthworm*, are missing. This omission may be due in part at least to his reliance on voluntary contributors in place of extensive fieldwork; untrained volunteers are far more likely to report on the extraordinary than on the ordinary, more pedestrian vocabulary.

In spite of all these reservations, Wright's study is both interesting and scholarly and must still be considered required reading for anyone interested in the study of English dialects. The first volume includes an excellent dialect grammar. Furthermore, the *English Dialect Dictionary* had a powerful influence on the development of dialect research in England. In fact, many scholars believed that Wright's study was so thorough that no additional research was needed. The feeling was that the work had already been done by Ellis and Wright, the latter of whom said, we remember, that he wanted to record all of the dialect words in English. Fortunately, there were enough more scientifically minded people in England to launch Orton's study, which, happily enough, was conducted for the most part at the University of Leeds, in Wright's native Yorkshire. From what we know of Joseph Wright, it would have delighted him that his own work should be continued and updated at Leeds, and by a Yorkshireman at that.

## Survey of English Dialects

England was the last western country to undertake a linguistic atlas, and when the initiative did come, it did not come exclusively from within England itself. The first suggestion came from John Orr, professor of romance philology at the University of Edinburgh and a former student of Jules Gilliéron. Orr wanted to produce an atlas based on the model of the *Sprach- und Sachatlas* of Jaberg and Jud, but nothing serious came of his suggestion. Then, in 1946, Eugen Dieth, a professor of philology at Zurich, pressed the Philological Society to establish a committee to plan an atlas for the whole of Britain. The Philological Society did not take the initiative, but Dieth found a willing colleague in Harold Orton, then at the University of Sheffield and soon to be professor of English philology at the University of Leeds. Orton, by this time, was no beginner in English dialectology. He had already published several works on the subject, the most significant of which was his *Phonology of a South Durham Dialect* in 1933.

Dieth and Orton spent their first planning sessions in the summer of 1947 designing a questionnaire. By 1948, the questionnaire was ready for field testing, and the final version, after some five revisions, was published in 1952 by the Leeds Philosophical and Literary Society. The questionnaire was long by American standards and relatively short by most European ones. There were 1,095 numbered questions, and since there were at times "subquestions" as well, the total number ran to 1,270. The questions themselves were grouped into nine sections: (1) the farmstead, (2) cultivation, (3) animals, (4) nature, (5) the house and housekeeping, (6) the human body, (7) numbers, time, and the weather, (8) social activities, and (9) states, actions, and relations. There were 387 questions which elicited phonological information, 128 morphological questions, 730 lexical questions, and 77 syntactic questions (which brings the total to 1,322 and not 1,270, but there were a number of questions which served a dual function). Also, each question was framed in a very precise way, and each fieldworker was required to ask all of them in the manner prescribed.

Dieth and Orton worked together, first on the questionnaire and later on the first field recordings. Then, in 1956, came Dieth's untimely death. Orton writes of him (Orton 1960; quoted from Allen and Underwood 1971):

> During these 10 years he [Dieth] had come to work with me in Leeds at least once a year, and sometimes twice. A tremendous enthusiast for English philology, he was truly an inspiring colleague. His most fruitful work on the Survey undoubtedly went into the organisation and compilation of our questionnaire. It was for him a challenging, captivating task, one that he delighted in doing and into which he put all of his almost limitless physical and mental energy.
>
> . . . but he was destined never to realise his cherished ambition, namely the completion of the Atlas itself. He had only just started his Northern maps when he died. The loss to English Dialectology was a disaster; and my own debt to him is incalculable and permanent. [Pp. 231–32]

After Dieth's death, the burden of the dialect survey of England fell on Orton, who, as we shall see, guided the major phase of the *Survey of English Dialects* to its completion before his own death in 1975.

Orton himself pointed out that the questionnaire of the *SED* is heavily oriented toward the farmer and his domestic and social life and that occupations such as fishing and mining were essentially ignored by the fieldworkers. Orton argued, however, that since farming is universal in England and other occupations are more local in nature, the farmer and his family "and the farming community in general, best preserve regional dialect in England today" (Orton 1960, quoted from Allen and Underwood 1971:233). Orton's fieldworkers were also instructed to ignore towns, since Orton believed that the towns and cities were objects of future research, requiring field techniques different from those needed for a linguistic atlas. Furthermore, most of the informants were men, since, again according to Orton, "in this country men speak vernacular more frequently, more consistently and more genuinely than women" (Orton 1962:15). Also, most of the informants, the vast majority in fact, were more than sixty years of age. There were two additional requirements for informants: they had to have lived continuously in their communities and, important indeed for phonetic recording, they could have no speech impediments.

The questionnaire itself contained five types of questions: naming, completing, converting, talking, and reverse questions. They are illustrated below:

*Naming questions*
What do you call a dog with half a dozen breeds in it? *mongrel*
What am I doing now (imitate)? *drinking*

*Completing questions*
Never drop a tumbler on the floor, because it's bound to . . . *break*
A man who cannot see at all is . . . *blind*

*Converting questions*
Base form: When I have an apple I . . . it. *eat*
Conversions: Yesterday, when I had an apple, I . . . it. *ate*
Whenever I've had an apple, I have always . . . it. *eaten*

*Talking questions*
What can you make from milk? *butter, cheese*
What trees have you around here? *birch, oak, elder, willow*

*Reverse questions*
What's the *barn* for, and where is it?
What do you mean by *corn* in these parts?

The converting questions were used rarely, and then only to elicit irregular verbs. The talking question was also used sparingly (Orton never liked the name, by the way) and was always followed by specific questions to ensure the recording of the proper responses. There were only ten reverse questions in the questionnaire, and these were used to ascertain the semantic varieties of specific words. The vast majority of the questions involved the informants' either completing a sentence or naming a thing or an action.

Not surprisingly, when one considers that the questionnaire required approximately twenty hours to complete, a further criterion for informant selection was a person's willingness to sit through a long interview. Often fieldworkers were forced to use as many as four or even five informants in order to complete a single field record. Orton said that this aspect presented no serious problems and indeed was advantageous at times.

The fieldwork was carried out between 1950 and 1961. Since the Scots in 1949 initiated their own *Linguistic Atlas of Scotland (LAS)* at the University of Edinburgh under the direction of Angus McIntosh (see below), Orton and Dieth decided to concentrate on England only and to forgo the original plan to survey the whole of Britain. Interviews were conducted in all of the forty counties. The fieldworkers chose representative informants when they arrived in their specific areas, and a total of 311 localities were sampled, with one questionnaire completed in each.

During the actual interviewing, the fieldworkers transcribed in phonetics the informants' responses, following the same procedure that had been used for the American atlases. Unlike many of the American interviews, however, most of the English interviews were recorded using portable tape recorders in the field. At the end of every week, each of the nine fieldworkers asked a best informant to talk about his or her daily life and work. These conversations were recorded as well, and the best of them were dubbed onto twelve-inch gramophone records.

After the fieldwork was completed in 1961, the arduous task of editing began. As the editing progressed, it was decided to postpone editing an atlas, for the immediate future only, in favor of a less costly publication format. Consequently, Orton opted for publishing the transcriptions in list manuscripts; unlike the *LAUM*, however, the English materials contain the phonetic transcriptions themselves and were published according to the following schedule:

    A. *Introduction to the Survey of English Dialects*, by Harold Orton
       (1962)
    B. The *Basic Materials* (four volumes, each in three parts)
       1. *The Six Northern Counties and the Isle of Man*, by Harold Orton
          and Wilfred Halliday (1962–1963)
       2. *The West Midland Counties*, by Harold Orton and Michael
          Barry (1969–1971)
       3. *The East Midland Counties and East Anglia*, by Harold Orton
          and Phillip Trilling (1969–1971)
       4. *The Southern Counties*, by Harold Orton and Martyn F.
          Wakelin (1967–1968)

In each case, the volumes of the *Basic Materials* are organized so that
one can look up any particular item, for example, the different terms for
*left-handed*, and can find the list manuscript with the informants' responses keyed to their localities.

During the time that the editing of the first volume of the *Basic Materials* was in its final stages, Eduard Kolb, from Basel, took over the work
on the northern counties which had been initiated by Dieth. In 1964,
Kolb published the *Phonological Atlas of the Northern Region: The Six Northern Counties, North Lincolnshire and the Isle of Man*. The atlas contains, in
Kolb's words, "all the phonological features of the Northern dialect that
make a geographical pattern" (p. 12). Figures 2–14 and 2–15 illustrate
Kolb's mapping techniques for *wheel*. We notice in figure 2–14 that the
pronunciation of *wheel* with an initial /hw-/, the preference of most
American school grammars, is restricted to the far North and to the Isle
of Man. Figure 2–15 shows the different vowels transcribed by the
fieldworkers.

The lexical material from the *SED* was analyzed by Orton and Nathalia Wright and was published in *A Word Geography of England* (1974). In
the introduction to the volume, Orton discusses many of the more than
220 maps and sometimes is able to draw parallels between the English
results and those of Kurath in the *Word Geography of the Eastern United
States*. There are, in fact, twenty-five words in the *Word Geography of
England* which also appear in the American worksheets, but generally,
however, there seems to have been only a minimum effort on the part of
the English to coordinate their efforts with the earlier American work.
On the other hand, it has always been true that dialectal variety in
England is far richer than that in North America; the following maps,
figures 2–16 and 2–17, showing the different terms for *left-handed*,
clearly illustrate this point. Nowhere in the American records is there
such a wealth of lexical variation.

The latest publication based on the materials of the *SED* is *The Linguis-*

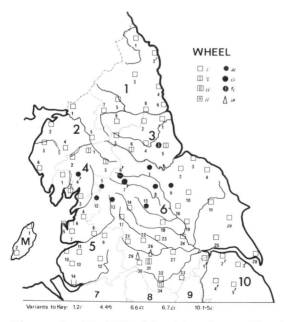

The long vowels: ME ē₁

## Wheel
OE *hweogol, hwēol, hwēl*

*Questionnaire*
i.9.5 What do you call this?

*Not asked*
5.12; 6.23 (map forms from
*wheel-wright* viii.4.4)

*Supplementary forms*
From viii.4.4: 3.5ḗ₁

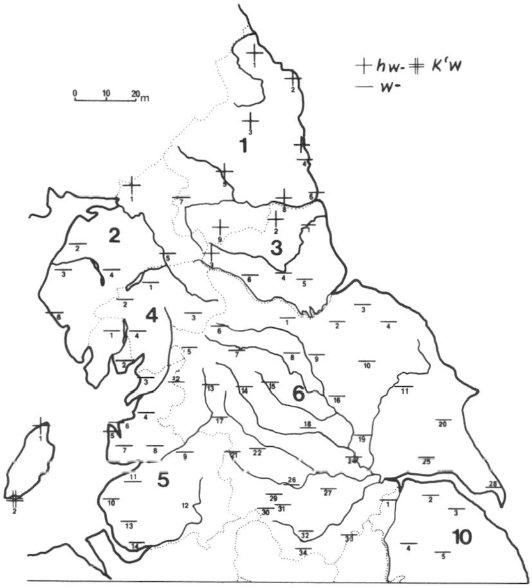

*Comparative list*
*wheel-* in *wheel-wright* vii.4.4. Divergences: *3.5* ᵉɩ; *3.6* ¹*i:*; *5.2 i:*; *6.6* ɥ*i*; *6.7 i:*;
*6.14* ¹*i:*; *6.29 i:*; *M.2*¹*i:*
*wheel-* not found at: *1.3–7,9; 2.2–5; 3.1; 4.4; 6.8,9,21,22,26; M.1*

*Figure 2–14. Wheel* in Northern England (Initial Consonant).
*Source*: Kolb 1964:172.

*Figure 2–15. Wheel* in Northern England (Vowels). *Source*:
Kolb 1964:173.

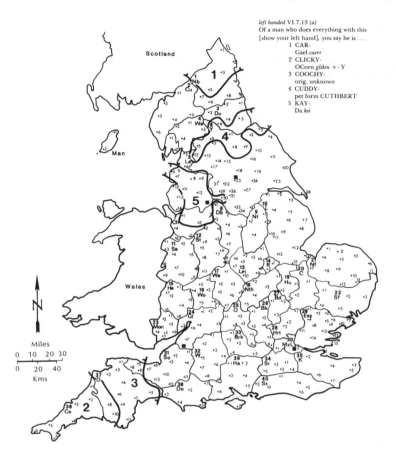

The word combined with the hyphenated words in the legend is HANDED (OE
*hand* + -ED).

CAR-PAWED (− + OF *powe* 13.. + -ED) 1Nb.2

CLICK 36Co.5; 36Co.7 left-hander

CLICKY 36Co.1/ [+]2/3/4/6, 37D8

COOCHY 37D.1–5/7/9

COOCHY-GAMMY (− + orig obsc 1879) 37D. [+]5; -PAWED (− + OF *powe* 13..
    + -ED) 37D. [+]7

CUDDY, 4We.4 left-hander

CUDDY-WIFTER (− + ? + -ER) 3Du.4/5 left-hander

KAY-FISTED (− + OE *fȳst* + -ED) 5La.5–8/11; -PAWED 5La.9/12, 7Ch.1–3;
    -NIEVED (− + ON *(h)nefi* 1300 + -ED) 6Y.30; -NIEVE 6Y. [+]30

SCROOCHY 37D.11 (? error for or var of COOCHY Edd)

*Figure 2–16. Left-handed* in England: *Car-, Clicky-, Coochy-,
Cuddy-, Kay-. Source*: Orton and Wright 1974:184.

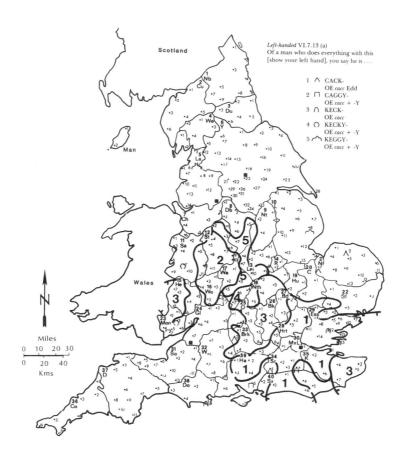

The word combined with the hyphenated words in both the legend and the notes is HANDED (OE *hand* + -ED) unless otherwise indicated.

CACKY (OE *cacc* + -Y Edd) 30MxL. [+1]

CAGGY-FISTED (− + OE *fýst* + -ED) 11Sa.8, 16Wo.4; -HAND (− + OE *hand*) 13Lei.7nd

CAT - 29Ess.4 (? error for CACK- Edd)

KECK-FISTED 15He.2/5/7, 23Mon.1/2

KECKY-FISTED 23Mon.3

KEGGY 12St.6

LEFT-KEGGY (OE *lyft* On + −) 10L.8, 12St. [+6/7], 16Wo. [+2]

*Figure 2–17. Left-handed* in England: *Cack-, Caggy-, Keck-, Kecky-, Keggy-. Source*: Orton and Wright 1974:185.

*tic Atlas of England* (*LAE*), by Orton, Stewart Sanderson, and John Widdowson (1978). This work appeared some three years after Orton's death, and although it admittedly does repeat some of the information published in earlier studies, it presents the data quite well. The book is divided into three sections: phonology, lexicon, and grammar. Not surprisingly, the largest section is devoted to phonological maps; the lexicon had already been treated extensively in Orton's and Wright's *Word Geography of England*. The grammatical materials are not mapped but rather presented in list form.

Figure 2–18 shows a fairly typical map from the *LAE*. In many ways, the cartographic principles here resemble those in the *LANE*, but of course there are important differences. The authors of the *LAE* draw isoglosses as best they can and then put within the various areas bounded by isoglosses the variant pronunciations elicited by the fieldworkers. Additional information which could not be entered on the maps was placed at the bottom of the page. In the case of *faint* in figure 2–18, for example, we see that informant 8 in Northumberland (area 1) used [e·ᵊ] instead of the [e:] indicated on the map. Similarly, informants 3 and 6 from Northumberland used [e:ᵊ] instead of [e:], and informants 6 from Durham (area 3) and 34 from Yorkshire (area 6) also used [e:ᵊ] rather than the [eə] prevalent in those two counties.

In a real sense, then, the publication of the *LAE* meant that the *Basic Materials* had been plumbed rather fully and that the project begun in the 1940s had essentially reached its conclusion. Scholars interested in dialectal variation in England have the relevant data at their disposal. The only other work based on the *Basic Materials* is Eduard Kolb's *Atlas of English Sounds* (1979), but it is not, strictly speaking, part of the *SED* project. It does add phonological maps to those produced in the *LAE*, but there is much repetition as well.

## *Survey of English Dialects* and the American Projects: A Comparison

A comparison of the *LAE* on the one hand and the American atlas projects on the other reveals interesting similarities and differences. First, both employed fieldworkers who transcribed the informants' responses during the actual interviews. Second, both emphasized the language of people who live in rural areas. Third, just about everything else about the two is different, including the informants themselves and the questionnaires and field techniques employed.

We noted that the American projects interviewed three different types

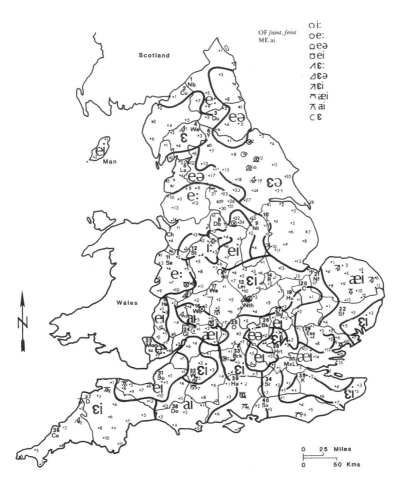

e·ᵊ 1Nb8, e:ᵊ 1Nb 3/6, 3Du6, 6Y 34,
    ę:ᵊ14 18Nth + 2 under eə
e:ɩ 16Wo3, 23Mon 1, e:ˡ 8Db3/5, 9Nt2, 11Sa 8,
    15He 2/5, 25Oχ 5, ę:ᵗ 8Db 7, ęɩə Man 1 under ei
ɛ:ɩ 11Sa + 10, ɛɩᵊ 16Wo2, ɛɩᵊ 20C2 under ɛi


ɩ 2Cu 3                    FAINTED pp 11 Sa +10; pt 3Du 2, 6Y7,
ɩə 3Du 1. 25Oχ 2              18Nth +2, 21Nf11; FAINTING ndg 29Ess6;
ɒɩ 15He 6                  FAINTY adj 32W 7, 34Sr3, 40Sχ 6


*Figure 2–18. LAE: Faint. Source*: Orton, Sanderson, and
Widdowson 1978:160.

of informants and thus provided scholars with an opportunity to make some sociolinguistic comparisons based on the field records. The *SED*, on the other hand, included mainly what in the United States and Canada would have been type I-A informants. Furthermore, although the *SED* does provide biographies of the informants, often very little linguistic information is listed; instead, we learn interesting facts about the people interviewed.

The worksheets of the various American projects give only the words which the fieldworker is to elicit from the informant, with occasional suggestions as to how the term should be elicited. The *SED* questionnaire included the form in which the questions were to be asked and required the fieldworkers to use only the form listed. These approaches have both positive and negative aspects. The American system allows each fieldworker to frame his own questions in the course of a relaxed conversation, and this flexibility could lead to a certain amount of semantic confusion. We do not know that we have complete parallelism for, to take one example, the names of plants in the American studies; *poison ivy* and *poison oak* are two different plants in some parts of the United States and two variant names for the same plant in other parts. The English method, because the questions are framed so as to demand specific answers, requires that each informant provide answers to the same questions, and thus the comparison between field records is made easier. On the other hand, American fieldworkers have found that each interview is special and requires a special approach, an exercise in interpersonal relations. As such, the freedom given to the American fieldworkers to elicit the responses in a conversation may have allowed them to use their initiative to make the interviews more productive. Clearly, both methods have their advantages, and it is frankly difficult to choose between them.

The length of the English questionnaire, as we have seen, made the fieldworkers' job more difficult insofar as informant selection was concerned, and often more than two informants were needed to complete one interview of approximately twenty hours' duration. In the United States and Canada, since an interview took only one-third that time, the ratio is almost one informant to one field record. Orton argued that the use of more than one informant does not bias the results of the *SED*, but some Americans have disagreed.

We noted that the *Handbook of the Linguistic Geography of New England* contains a comparison and a critique of the fieldworkers. The *LAUM* contains a similar section, but no such information is provided by the *SED*. Since no fieldworker is strong in all areas of fieldwork, it is truly unfortunate that the English did not decide to follow the American example in this respect. A look at the *Basic Materials* for Leicestershire and Rutland reveals that Averil H. Playford did not record very many nonstandard grammatical forms. It is of course possible that those informants did not use such forms in their everyday speech, but it is far more probable that the fieldworker simply was weaker in that area of linguistic interviewing.

One of the greatest advantages the English study has over the American ones is that the portable tape recorder was used consistently in the former. The more recent American fieldwork, such as that for the *Linguistic Atlas of the Gulf States*, has also been tape-recorded.

Another rather striking difference between the English and the American approaches is their differing definitions of the term *dialect*. We saw that for the Americans, and for us as well, *dialect* is synonymous with *variety of language*, standard or nonstandard. Dialect in the *SED* clearly means a nonstandard variety of English, different from the London standard. When we consider the changing status of RP in England (see above), this may not have been a wise decision on the part of the *SED*. Moreover, the decision to interview more men than women in England may also be questionable. Orton's assertion that men speak more nonstandard English than women may not be true. We do know that of the *LAUM*'s 208 informants, there were 88 women, 37 of whom were type I, 45 of whom were type II, and 6 of whom were type III. It may be, of course, that the linguistic situations in England and America are different, but then we should require some proof that this is so. An assertion is not enough.

One of the more interesting aspects of the two studies concerns their omissions. In spite of the length of the *SED* questionnaire, it has comparatively few lexical items which also exist in the worksheets of the American atlas projects. For this reason, many scholars have not been able to make some kinds of comparisons concerning the sources of American English terms. It is possible, of course, to argue that the English sought to do the best job they could on their own varieties of English and that American problems should not have been relevant to them. In any case, the twenty-five cases where the *SED* questionnaire and the American worksheets overlap provide too few opportunities for adequate comparison of the two projects at the lexical level.

Raven I. McDavid, Jr., in a review of the *SED* (McDavid 1971) states the case as follows:

> . . . even in the domain of unquestioned folk speech there are omissions in the English questionnaire that keep students from making as effective comparisons as they might between English and American usage. Among items not recorded in England are the names for the *earthworm* and the *dragonfly*, and the past tense of *climb*, *dive*, and *rise*. [Pp. 29, 34]

It is possible that the terms cited by McDavid are not viable dialect terms in England, but there is no way for us to be sure.

## Linguistic Atlas of Scotland

The dialect survey of Scotland, launched in the early 1950s, has appeared thus far in two volumes, in 1975 and 1977. It is based on principles rather different from those of its English and American cousins, however, in that one of the goals of the *Linguistic Atlas of Scotland* is to find structural relationships between dialects (see chapter 4, "The Search for a Structural Dialectology"). In 1952, Angus McIntosh, the director of the *LAS*, published his *Introduction to a Survey of Scottish Dialects* and discussed this principle in detail. The questionnaire used by the Scots contains 907 purely phonological items, chosen because they represent vowels and consonants in specific linguistic contexts. For example, each vowel is elicited before the sounds /t/ and /d/ and at the ends of words as well. The concentration on vowels, says McIntosh, is a function of the fact that they vary more than consonants do, and here, of course, McIntosh reiterates both the English and the American point of view. In addition to the phonological part of the questionnaire, there are 75 grammatical items, mainly intended to reveal nonstandard verb forms and a few nonstandard noun plurals.

The lexical part of the Scottish questionnaire brings us, to some extent at least, back to Georg Wenker. McIntosh used a postal questionnaire, mailed to every school in Scotland. On the other hand, there are significant differences between Wenker's technique and McIntosh's, the most fundamental being the kind of information elicited by the questionnaire. Whereas Wenker tried to elicit phonological information, the *LAS*, following the lead provided by A. L. Davis's unpublished doctoral dissertation, "A Word Atlas of the Great Lakes Region," tried to elicit almost exclusively lexical data. In other words, instead of asking informants to write in some kind of phonetic alphabet, the *LAS*, like Davis's study before it, asked for different *words* for different things. In the cases where the *LAS* questionnaire did ask for phonological information, its technique was far different from Wenker's. It asked questions such as "Is *ch* pronounced *sh* in CHEW?" [I, p. 428]. Each questionnaire was answered by an informant who was a native of his area and who had at least one parent also born in the same area. The phonological data mentioned earlier were elicited by direct fieldwork.

Like all its predecessors, the *LAS* will contain data on phonology, lexicon, and grammar, but its mapping techniques are different from those of the atlases discussed in this chapter. First of all, page-sized maps

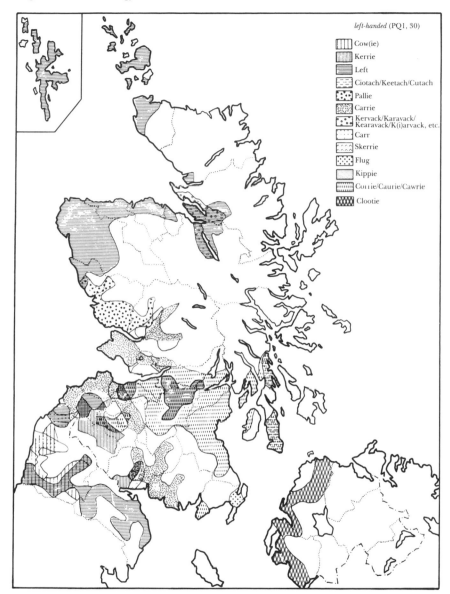

*Figure 2–19. LAS: Left-handed (Map). Source:* Mather and Speitel 1975:I:36.

## 6 LEFT HANDED ((PQ1, 30)

Map 6 [figure 2–19] shows the distribution of the elements meaning *left*, map 6A those of *handed*. The compound forms are not mapped because the picture is rather confusing. On map 6A the SE form *handed* has not been shown as it occurs nearly everywhere.

The variants of HANDED (*hannit, hawndit, hant,* etc.) have been subsumed. The endings -it, -ed in *clueked, cleukit, clucket, jookit, jooked,* etc., have been subsumed under the majority spelling of such items in each county.

*Shetland*
Kag handed—24
Left handed—1–4, 6–8, 10, 13, 15–17, 19, 21ab, 25, 27, 30, 32–33
Left (maig)—5, 20
Maeg handed—9
Squint handed—23
Wrang handed—14, 26
Nil—11–12, 18, 22, 28–29, 31
*Orkney*
Left handed—1–5, 7–9, 11, 13ab, 16–17, 19–21
Pardie pawed—16
Nil—6, 10, 12, 14–15, 18
*Caithness*
Carrie handed—12b
Corrie fisted—15
Corrie handed—6, 12b, 16a
Left handed—2ab, 8–9, 11, 13–14, 16b
Left mitted—12a
Left spoke—5
Left spound—4
Left spung—8
Wrong handed—13
Nil—1, 3, 7, 10, 12c, 17
*Sutherland*
Corrie fisted—5
Corrie (handed)—9ab
Corrie juked—8
Karisbag—12
Karispogue—10, 15
Kerrack—14
Kervack—8
Left handed—1, 3–4, 6–8, 10–13, 16–17
Leftie—3, 16
Nil—2
*Ross & Cromarty*
Carrie fisted—34
Carrie handed—11
Caurie fisted—17
Corrie fisted—20, 25a

Corrie handed—24
Garvack—8
Karavack—17, 28, 31
Kearack—3
Kearavack—32b
Kearvack—7, 23
Kerivack—12, 27
Kervack—35
Kervag—14
Kervie—13
Kiarvack—10
Kippie—18
Kyarvack—18, 20
Left handed—1, 3–5, 9–10, 16–17, 19, 24, 25b, 26–27, 29–31, 32ab, 36, 39
Left mellett—37a
Left pawed—25b
Nil—2, 6, 15, 21–22, 32c, 33, 37b, 38
*Inverness*
Carie handed—9, 22
Corrie fisted—38, 40
Corrie handed—24, 31, 33, 37
Kairack—24
Karvack—20
Kearack—31
Kearag—13d
Kerrack—14
Kiarack—13ace
Kiotach—26
Kwarach—13b
Left handed—1–6, 8–9, 11–12, 13ce, 16–19, 21ab, 22–23, 25–30, 32–37, 39–40
Leftie—14
Nil—7, 10, 15
*Nairn*
Corrie fisted—1b
Corrie handed—2
Garroch—1b
Guarrach—1c
Kiarack—1a
Left handed—2, 6

Nil—3–5

*Moray*
Carie fisted—6a
Corbie—22
Corrie fisted—12, 22
Corrie handed—18
Corvie fisted—21
Kargarack—22
Kiarrack—8d
Left cleuched—2b, 3, 5, 9a, 16, 18
(Left) cleukit—1, 22
Left clooched—4, 6b, 15
Left clookit—6a, 7, 8b, 9a, 10, 19–21
Left handed—4, 6b, 7, 11, 14
Left spyogued—13
Lett clouch—8e
Nil—2a, 8acf, 9b, 17, 23

*Banff*
Carrie handed—33
Caurie handed—27
Conter handed—23
Corrie fisted—11, 14–15
Currie fisted—18d
Kair cuekit—1, 2bc, 3
Left cleekit—11
Left clewkit—14–15, 20, 30
Left clookit—3–5, 6ab, 7, 9–10, 12, 16–17, 18b, 19, 21–25, 27, 31–32, 34
Left handed—8–9, 13, 16, 18c
Left hewkit—2a, 4, 6a
Left kewkit—2b
Left mitted—18b
Left puttett—17, 18b
Maukin—33
Nil—18a, 26, 28–29

*Figure 2–20. LAS: Left-handed* (List Manuscript). *Source:* Mather and Speitel 1977:II:161–162.

are presented for all relevant lexical items, and rather than drawing isoglosses, as the *LAE* did, or printing transcriptions, as did the *LANE*, the *LAS* shaded areas on the maps, as in figure 2–19. In addition to these maps, however, the *LAS* also contains the list manuscripts for all of the informants' responses to the items on the questionnaire. Figure 2–20 presents part of the list of responses which accompany the map of *left-handed* in figure 2–19. The list manuscript is surely easy to read. We see that, in Shetland County, only informant 24 used the term *kag handed*, that informant 9 used the form *maeg handed*, and so on. For comparative purposes, the reader here might want to turn back to figures 2–16 and 2–17, the maps of *left-handed* in the *Word Geography of England*. Only the lexical data of the *LAS* have been published as of this writing.

## Dialect Geography under Attack: Glenna R. Pickford and Gary N. Underwood

We have now completed our survey of the major linguistic atlases and their allied projects. We have seen that both the British and American atlases focus primarily on folk speech, on the speech of the relatively uneducated members of the rural speech community. The typical American position on the *SED* is that the singular focus on folk speech in England is too myopic, and the Americans have been quick to point out that the various American projects have included informants in urban areas. At the same time, and for reasons already discussed here, nearly all American dialectologists have also admitted that they, too, have interviewed the vast majority of their informants in rural areas. In recent years, this procedure has come under attack, first by a sociologist and then by one of the younger generation of dialectologists.

In 1956, the sociologist Glenna R. Pickford published "American Linguistic Geography: A Sociological Appraisal" and attacked just about everything having to do with the *LANE*, the only American linguistic atlas then published. She found fault with the *LANE*'s methods of sampling informants, its worksheets, and the validity of Kurath's and others' conclusions about the nature of American speech. Pickford's major premise was that in an extraordinarily mobile society such as that in North America, geography is not the important factor in linguistic diversity that it is in the once-peasant societies of Europe or England, which are far more stable.

Without analyzing her criticisms in detail, we can take a few of Pickford's major points to see the general focus of her attack. She noted that the *LANE* planners took no account whatever of modern sampling techniques, and to the extent that the findings aim to be representative, their results are invalid. She argues that dialect geographers do not use a *random sample* (chapter 3), where each person in the total population has some chance of being selected, and she also points out that the quantitative methods used by some dialectologists are invalid because of the absence of such a sample. We will discuss the problem of sampling in chapter 3, but for now it is enough to point out that dialect geographers everywhere—in Europe, Britain, and North America—have always used a *judgment sample*, where informants are chosen because they meet certain criteria, for example, being older, uneducated, and native to the areas in which they live.

Pickford argues that even the judgment sample of the *LANE* is inadequate, since it does not reflect the speech of the total population. The informants chosen were only those who would agree to sit for an interview lasting about six to eight hours, and this requirement, according to Pickford, biased the sample. There were no safeguards built into the *LANE* to determine whether those who did not agree to be informants were somehow different in their speech habits from those who did agree. Pickford also argues that the informants for the *LANE* came from communities which, for the most part, were "culturally subordinate" and were not the major population centers. In other words, Kurath and his colleagues, according to Pickford, did not put sufficient stress on the process of urbanization, a process which has been under way since colonial times in North America.

Perhaps Pickford's most damning criticism of the methods of American dialectologists concerns informant selection and typing. She argues that no sociologist would ever have based informant types on education alone, as the American dialectologists did. Their class distinctions, Pickford argues, are primitive in the extreme, and here as well as in other places in her article she laments the fact that the planners of the *LANE* did not consult with experts in the field of sociology before they began the process of interviewing.

Pickford noted that sampling the oldest living native of a community, something which the American fieldworkers have always tried to do, does not give us an accurate picture of American speech. People move about in the United States more than they do anywhere else in the world. In California, for example, the natives are in such a minority that their speech in no way can be said to represent the speech of the state in which they live. On the other hand, the native of Carcassonne probably comes from a family which has lived in that community for generations, and so that person is more representative of a class.

Pickford concludes that the *LANE* is not a vehicle by which we can understand better the phenomenon of American dialects. The informants are not necessarily representative of the speech of their communities, and the communities sampled are not representative of the American scene. Bluntly put, the speech recorded by the American fieldworkers is not representative of American speech in all its complexity.

Pickford's criticisms did not go unanswered by linguistic geographers. McDavid has frequently observed that the aim of linguistic atlas projects is not, as Pickford maintained, to present a representative and complete picture of the complexity of the speech patterns of the United States and Canada; rather, the *LANE* tried to do exactly what Pickford says it does do: to describe the more or less stable speech of the people in rural areas, of people who are essentially sedentary. That is, according to McDavid, Pickford really did not understand the basic principles underlying the *LANE*. McDavid (1972) noted:

> Whatever the current mode of interest in dialects may be, it is none the less true that the primary purpose of a linguistic atlas is that of historical linguistics, of providing a body of stable folk evidence, from which one may work backward, comparatively, to set up affiliations of the dialect regions with those in older settled areas and in the British Isles. [P. 37]

We could also point out that some of Pickford's criticisms of the *LANE* result from her perspective of some twenty-seven years. When *LANE* was planned, in 1929, sampling theory and techniques, as well as theories of social class, were not nearly as well developed as they were in 1956, when Pickford published her article. Since then, however, the American field records have indeed been used for much sociolinguistic analysis, and as yet no one has answered Pickford's criticisms of the way informants are typed. The *LAUM* was published in the 1970s and uses the same criteria that the *LANE* did more than thirty years earlier. It might well be argued that future studies, if they are to provide the basis for sociolinguistic conclusions, should be at least somewhat modernized with respect to the criteria for putting informants into types, even if they maintain their rural emphasis.

A criticism of the methods of American dialectology came from another direction in the early 1970s—from the ranks of the dialectologists themselves. Gary N. Underwood, then the director of the *Linguistic Atlas of the Southwest States*, came to the conclusion that there is no point in continuing to do atlas-type research of the traditional kind in the United States. He writes: "But in the past forty-two years since the inauguration to the *LANE* linguistics has advanced too far for us to continue to study dialects with a methodology that has not been significantly improved in half a century" (Underwood 1974:19).

Underwood seems to agree unreservedly with the criticisms of

Pickford and suggests that the whole methodology be scrapped: "Ling-uistic atlas methodology does not need to be modified; it needs to be abandoned and replaced by a new one if we are seriously interested in a realistic, accurate account of regional and social variation in American English" (Underwood 1974:20).

In discussing atlas interview techniques, Underwood argues that the fieldworker does more talking than the informant because the field-worker must elicit the desired forms. In fact, Underwood suggests that the very question technique makes the whole affair more like an ex-amination than like an interview, and thus the results may be biased. He gives us an example of questions, taken from the *Gulf States* atlas (Peder-son et al. 1972:161), and typical of those used by atlas fieldworkers: "A long thin-bodied insect, with a hard little beak and two pairs of shiny wings; it hovers around damp places and eats its own weight in mos-quitoes, etc." (Underwood 1974:27). The answer, of course, is *dragonfly*, or one of its equivalents, such as *snake doctor, snake feeder, (devil's) darning needle*, and so forth. Underwood's point is that the fieldworker produces a long sentence in order to draw one or two words from the informant.

The linguistic atlas interview is weak for another reason, says Underwood. It samples only one style of speech, even though we know today that each of us uses several styles (see chapter 3, "Social Dialectolo-gy"). Because the interview consists of direct questions from the fieldworker to the informant, with conversational forms being picked up in a fairly haphazard fashion, only one style is recorded. Moreover, an experienced fieldworker such as McDavid, who was skilled enough to elicit the requisite terms during a conversation, may have recorded a style of speech totally different from that recorded by fieldworkers who relied more closely on the question technique and operated in a manner similar to the one used for the *SED*.

Underwood also finds the worksheets of the American atlas projects to be unsatisfactory. In the most recent project, the *Linguistic Atlas of the Gulf States*, Underwood notes that we still find items such as calls to oxen, parts of a wooden wagon, shafts of a buggy, and so on. Furthermore, even at the inception of that project, according to Underwood, Amer-ican linguistic atlases had an "Anglo-Saxon bias." Since the starting point of the *LANE* consisted of articles in *Dialect Notes* and *American Speech* and Ellis's dialect test, there was no provision for sampling the speech of the ethnic minorities in North America.

Underwood sees a similar bias in the selection of informants. Only about fifty blacks were interviewed in the entire Atlantic coastal region. Underwood argues that even this disproportion would not be particu-larly wrong, given the stated aims of linguistic atlases: in McDavid's words, "the primary purpose of a linguistic atlas is that of historical linguistics" (1972:37). Often, however, Underwood sees some dialect geographers as exaggerating the nature of their findings. He quotes Kurath in the *Word Geography of the Eastern United States* (p. v): "This systematic record of the usage of more than 1200 persons gives us full information on the geographic and social dissemination of the words and the phrases selected for this study" (Underwood 1974:30). Certainly Kurath is far less modest in his characterization of atlas findings than was McDavid in the section quoted earlier.

Underwood (1974) concludes with some recommendations for the survey of English in the southwestern United States. He ends, however, on a rather gloomy note:

> The type of dialect research I envision for the Southwest not only calls for a combination of difficult field work and theoretical models, but also for cooperation between linguists of various talents and anthropologists, folklorists, sociologists, and perhaps psychologists. Even this tentative and crude sketch of the suggested research poses such formidable problems that the likelihood that such research will even be conducted may be extremely remote. That is no justification, however, for maintaining the *status quo* of mainstream [i.e., traditional] dialectology. [Pp. 36–37]

What is interesting here is that Underwood never really assesses the goal which McDavid sees for a linguistic atlas, that of providing a historical record. Instead, Underwood often attacks the American atlases for not doing what they never were designed to do. It is surely true that, for all practical purposes, the worksheets are designed so as to elicit only one style of speech: that which we use with a stranger with whom we are on fairly good terms. To conclude from this fact that all the atlas projects should be scrapped is hardly reasonable. Moreover, the *dragonfly* example is rather extreme; many fieldworkers showed pictures or a pencil sketch, and many other questions are much shorter.

Underwood's suggestion that skilled fieldworkers who were able to elicit forms in a fairly relaxed conversation were recording styles different from those noted by less experienced fieldworkers may give the reader the false impression that many of the fieldworkers were inexperienced. This is simply not the case, but even if it were, the two published American atlases (*LANE* and *LAUM*) include a ranking of fieldworkers, so that the reader can learn which ones best elicited conversational forms. The claims of some dialectologists notwithstanding, there are innumerable things that the atlas projects do not do, but then, what single scientific project ever answers all the questions there are to ask? Surely additional work needs to be done for, say, the upper Midwest after the publication of the *LAUM*; still, knowledge is cumulative. Since

Underwood does not find everything he would like to find in the American atlases, he would have us throw out the whole project.

Both Pickford and Underwood argue that linguistic geography is so far out of date that it should be abandoned in favor of more rewarding kinds of research. We can say at this point that several areas in atlas methodology could indeed be modernized before additional work is carried out, but even that effort would mean losing something: the ability to make comparisons between the different regional atlases. Underwood notes that Pederson's Gulf States atlas includes terms for parts of wagons and buggies as well as calls to oxen. We should ask whether the informants for Pederson's study knew such terms; if they did, then why not ask them? By doing so, we can compare their responses to those of informants interviewed twenty or more years ago in other parts of the United States.

In spite of the attacks by Pickford and Underwood, it seems clear that the time and effort expended on the *LANE*, the *LAUM*, and other atlas projects have not been wasted altogether. On the other hand, like all large projects, the linguistic atlases in the United States and Canada and England do have their weak points. Clearly, Pickford's point that education may be given too high a value in the typing of informants is a good one, even though she offers no evidence and cites no wrong classifications of informants in *LANE*, but we must remember that, at least as far as the *LANE* is concerned, the study of class stratification was not well developed when it was planned. The same is not so true for the *LAUM*, but even here some of the fieldwork was completed thirty years ago. Changing the worksheets and/or informant selection and typing techniques would mean that opportunities for comparison would be lost. What we need, of course, are follow-up studies to fill in the gaps left by the various atlases. Such studies can build on the atlas work done previously.

Underwood is correct when he points out that the American worksheets are geared to rural informants, but then, even in more recent projects, such as Pederson's *Linguistic Atlas of the Gulf States*, these are the people the fieldworkers try to reach. Nothing prevents further study of urban speech, and in fact the *Linguistic Atlas of the Gulf States* docs include an "Urban Supplement" (Billiard and Pederson 1979). It is also true that the Anglo-Saxon bias noted by Underwood exists in the worksheets and that too few blacks have been interviewed in many atlas projects, but additional study should correct this imbalance.

We would also do well to remember that most linguistic atlases in North America and in England have gathered huge amounts of data, but with a few exceptions only, there have never been enough people or enough financial resources to perform analyses quickly and to prepare them for publication. For this reason, any atlas project published in the last decades of this century will be very out of date in terms of its description of American speech. Atlases will, however, provide excellent data for historical and comparative studies.

Another more serious problem with both the American atlases and the *SED* has been noted orally by Macklin Thomas of Chicago State University. Thomas, a statistician, observed that the data for such studies are "irretrievable." That is, there is no way to go back and check the accuracy of the transcriptions. Are the different pronunciations of the vowels in, for example, the *LAUM* or the *LAE* a function of informant behavior or of fieldworker behavior? We have to assume that they relate to the former, but we can never really know for sure. Not all of the recordings exist in their entirety.

In summary, then, both the American atlas projects and the *SED* have their flaws. We have seen, however, that much can be learned from them, providing that we bear in mind their shortcomings when we use the works themselves. One need not leave dialectology in favor of theology after noticing that nothing under the sun is ever perfect; science, too, has recognized this truth for a long time. Flaws in one study can be remedied up to a point by the next study, for by "standing on the shoulders" of previous workers scientists extend knowledge in every field. Surely the various atlases and other works surveyed in this chapter have taken us a long way in that never-ending pursuit.

## Bibliographical Note

On the beginnings in Europe, see Moulton (1972) and Pop (1950). The major sources for the discussion of the *LANE* and its backgrounds are Kurath (1939) and McDavid (1958). The sources for the backgrounds of the *SED* are Mencken (1963), Moulton (1972), Orton (1960, 1962), and Wakelin (1972).

# 3

# *Social Dialectology*

## Some Elementary Statistics

We saw in the last chapter that many of Pickford's criticisms of the *LANE* were based on the idea that the sample of informants drawn for that study was somehow biased and thus did not adequately represent the speech of New England. Many of Underwood's criticisms had the same focus. In order to understand these arguments better and, perhaps more important, in order to evaluate the research in social dialectology which began in earnest in the middle years of the 1960s, we need some understanding of the methods used to evaluate linguistic results that are quantitative. For example, when we looked at the *LAUM*, we noted that some results were presented in terms of percentages, but how can we interpret the meaning of the numbers in figure 2–13? We shall see that simply looking at numbers is often not enough; we need statistical tests to evaluate them.

To state the matter quite simply, statistics helps us to (1) gather, (2) organize and classify, and (3) evaluate the reliability of data. As far as (1) is concerned, we enter the realm of *sampling*, which may take several forms. That used by all the atlases in the last chapter is usually called a *judgment sample*: a fieldworker goes into an assigned area and finds informants who meet certain criteria. Pickford described the problems with such a sample, noting that there is a chance that informants so selected may not be representative of the population involved. She suggested a *random sample*, where everyone in the population has a chance of being selected.

In spite of the name, a random sample is anything but a haphazard choosing of informants for a study. The classic way to sample randomly would be to list all the people in a population; if there were a total of 1,000,000 people and we wanted a sample of 1,000, we would choose every thousandth name on the list. Such a procedure can be expensive, and even if one has the money, there is often no way to obtain a complete list of a population. Not everyone pays taxes, so tax rolls are no good. Not everyone has a telephone, and many married women are listed under their husbands' names, so we cannot use the telephone book. In fact, a true random sample is extraordinarily difficult to achieve in linguistic research, and even if we could make one, there would be additional problems. For example, how could we guarantee that everyone chosen for the random sample would have a complete set of front teeth? We would not be able to use an informant lacking teeth for the study of certain phonetic phenomena, and if we replaced even one person by someone else, the sample would no longer be random.

On the other hand, all American linguistic atlas fieldwork has employed a kind of judgment sample called a *stratified*, or *quota, sample*. That is, the informants have been chosen so as to fit into several categories of age and education, and the researcher must then take precautions to ensure that the sample is not biased: that both sexes, all relevant age groups, and so on are equally represented. But here we have a problem, because all statistical tests are designed to be valid only when the sample is random. In fact, since statistical tests are based on the theory of probability, another name for random sample is *probability sample*. So what choice do we have? We can make a temporary presupposition that our *sample* is, in fact, the whole *population*; then we can use statistical tests, but we must never lose sight of the fact that our results are valid only for our sample, and another study could conceivably produce results different from ours. This chance we must take, and as we shall see later in this chapter, all research in social dialectology does so as well. No study to date has used a strictly random sample; instead, workers have taken as many precautions as possible to ensure that their judgment samples are not biased. The most common way of preventing bias is to make the judgment sample from a previously chosen random sample. If the original random sample was a good one, then we can perhaps assume that choosing people from it who are, for example, native speakers of English will not bias the sample for the linguistic research.

The question most frequently asked concerning sampling is, of course, "How big a sample?" Although Gallup uses about 1,600 informants, most linguistic studies to date have used as few as 88 (Labov 1966), 36 (Shuy 1968), and 60 (Wolfram 1969). Unfortunately, there is no clear prescription for sample size, even though some statistics books do give formulas. Of course, we could actually do the research and then follow it with another study on a different sample to see if the two sets of findings are different, but as yet no linguist has done so.

Clearly, however, if we want our results to be reliable for a certain population, we must sample carefully from that population. We cannot use a study of the speech of Minneapolis to make conclusions about the speech of St. Paul, in spite of the close geographic proximity of the two cities. Sampling theory demands that we sample the speech of St. Paul in order to draw conclusions about that city's speech.

Assuming, however, that we do have a good sample, how can we then organize our data for evaluation? The most common method is a *frequency distribution*, simply a list of scores organized from the highest to the lowest, as shown below.

| Child number | Age |
|:---:|:---:|
| 1 | 8 |
| 2 | 6 |
| 3 | 5 |
| 4 | 4 |
| 5 | 2 |

Once we have a frequency distribution, a number of calculations are possible. For example, we might want to know the average age of the children, so we simply add up the total ages and divide by the number of children. That gives us a *mean*, or arithmetic average, of 5. But sometimes the mean can be misleading; for example, if three people have daily incomes of $5.00, $11.00, and $500,000.00, respectively, their mean daily income is $166,672, but that figure clearly lacks meaning for the sample, since one person is fabulously rich and the other two are quite poor.

For this reason, we need another calculation, called the *standard deviation*. Generally speaking, the standard deviation is a measure of the degree to which each element in a frequency distribution deviates from the mean. In fact, it is the average deviation of each element from the mean. A fuller explanation of the term is beyond the scope of this book; it is enough to know that the standard deviation measures the spread between the various scores. To calculate standard deviation (or $s$), we subtract each score ($X_i$) from the mean ($m$), square the result, add up ($\Sigma$ denotes *sum*) all the squares, divide that sum by the number of elements minus one ($N - 1$) in the frequency distribution itself, and then take the square root of the total. The formula, then, is:

$$s = \sqrt{\dfrac{\sum\limits_{i=1}^{N} (X_1 - m)^2}{(N - 1)}}$$                    (Ex. 3–1)

The calculation of $s$ can be illustrated using the children with a mean age of 5.

|        | $X_i$     | $(X_i - m)$ | $(X_i - m)^2$ |
|--------|-----------|-------------|---------------|
| 1.     | 8         | 3           | 9             |
| 2.     | 6         | 1           | 1             |
| 3.     | 5         | 0           | 0             |
| 4.     | 4         | −1          | 1             |
| 5.     | 2         | −3          | 9             |
|        | $N = 5$   |             | $\Sigma (X_i - m)^2 = 20$ |

$$s = \sqrt{\dfrac{20}{4}}$$

$$s = \sqrt{5}$$

$$s = 2.24$$                    Ex. 3–2

So we see that the children have a mean age of 5 and a standard deviation of 2.24; that is, the age of each child, on the average, differs from the mean by 2.24 years. In the case of the three incomes with a mean of $166,672, we can also calculate the standard deviation; if we do so, we learn that it is a whopping $288,670.00—a clear indication that our data are widely spread and not homogeneous. We do not have to be concerned with why $s$ works, but it is important to know that $s$ is used in many statistical tests for the reliability of results. It is also worth noting that if each score in a frequency distribution is the same, the standard deviation will be zero; the mean will be the same as each individual score, and $(X_i - m)$ in the formula will be zero.

We now know how to begin to evaluate data. We can calculate the mean and standard deviation of a frequency distribution, and we can evaluate those results to some extent at least. The standard deviation has another property, however, which is extremely helpful. Given the laws of probability, and given a sample larger than thirty (for reasons which need not concern us here), a distance of one standard deviation on each side of the mean will cover approximately 68 percent of all the cases in a sample. That is, if we have a sample with a mean of 125 and a standard deviation of 12, then 68 percent of all the cases in our frequency distribution will fall somewhere between 113 (125 − 12) and 137 (125 + 12). Similarly, approximately two standard deviations left and right of the mean cover 95 percent of the scores, or in the above case, 101 (125 − 24) to 149 (125 + 24). This property of *s*, as we shall see, is quite useful, because it means that if we have results that are more than two standard deviations left and right of the mean, we can be 95 percent certain that those results are valid.

Once the mean and standard deviation are known, we are in a position to answer a very important question: how do we determine whether the difference between the two means is significant? Suppose, for example, that the mean score of twenty-five students on one test is 65, with a standard deviation of 15, whereas the mean score of the same students on the next test is 70, with a standard deviation of 12. Can we say, automatically, that the students improved? Not until the results are evaluated using a statistical test, and the test is quite simple. We take the squares of the two standard deviations, divide them by the number of students in the two samples, add the results, and take the square root. Then we divide that number into the actual difference between the means and see if the result is at least 1.96. The formula for the test is as follows, where $m_1$ is the mean of one frequency distribution, and $m_2$ is the mean of the other; $s_1$ is the standard deviation of the first mean, and $s_2$ is that of the other; $z$ is the actual number we are looking for, to see if it is at least 1.96.

$$z = \frac{m_1 - m_2}{\sqrt{\dfrac{s_1^2}{N_1} + \dfrac{s_2^2}{N_2}}}$$

(Ex. 3–3)

The problem of the examination scores noted above can then be solved.

$$z = \frac{65 - 70}{\sqrt{\dfrac{15^2}{25} + \dfrac{12^2}{25}}}$$

$$z = \frac{5}{\sqrt{\dfrac{225}{25} + \dfrac{144}{25}}}$$

$$z = \frac{5}{\sqrt{14.76}}$$

$$z = \frac{5}{3.84}$$

$$z = \quad 1.30 \qquad\qquad\qquad\qquad\qquad \text{(Ex. 3–4)}$$

Since $z$ is an absolute number, the minus sign does not matter (and has been deleted). We see that the results of the test fall below the minimum of 1.96, so, given our desire for 95 percent certainty, we conclude that the difference between the two examination scores is not significant. Of course, if we desired to be less certain, we could use a lower number than 95 percent, but that is generally the minimum confidence level acceptable to statisticians in the social sciences. Some even insist on a 99 percent figure, and then the $z$ score must be at least 2.58, given the laws of probability.

In another case, the mean age of 100 sampled houses in Chicago is 23 years with a standard deviation of 4, and the mean age of 50 sampled houses in Detroit is 21 years with a standard deviation of 5. Is this difference of 2 years significant at our 95 percent level of confidence? Here $m_1 = 23$, $m_2 = 21$, $s_1 = 4$, $s_2 = 5$, $N_1 = 100$, and $N_2 = 50$.

$$z = \frac{23 - 21}{\sqrt{\dfrac{4^2}{100} + \dfrac{5^2}{50}}}$$

$$z = \frac{2}{\sqrt{.66}}$$

$$z = \frac{2}{.812}$$

$$z = \quad 2.46 \qquad\qquad\qquad\qquad\qquad \text{(Ex. 3–5)}$$

In this case, even though the difference between the two means is only 2 years, it is indeed significant at the 95 percent level of confidence, but since the calculated $z$ is less than 2.58, we did not reach a confidence level of 99 percent.

Statisticians usually express these kinds of confidence levels in slightly different terms. That is, they call the 95 percent level of confidence $p < .05$, meaning that there is still a 5 percent probability that the difference between the two means is the result of chance alone. We said that we were 95 percent certain; the statistician opts for the reverse formulation, being 5 percent *unsure* of the results. This difference may seem trivial, but from here on, we, too, will use the general statistical expression and will say that the difference between the mean ages of the houses was significiant at $p < .05$ but that the difference between the examination scores was not so.

We have just been looking at statistical tests where the samples involved are more than thirty in number. Generally speaking, the larger the sample, the more accurate it is, if it is chosen carefully, of course. Many times in linguistic research, however, sample sizes are smaller, and we need different tests to measure the significance of results. In the case of the difference between two means, the test is called a *t-test*, and its formula is similar to the one in example 3–3, with additional elements.

$$t = \frac{m_1 - m_2}{\sqrt{\frac{(N_1 - 1)s_1^2 + (N_2 - 1)s_2^2}{(N_1 + N_2 - 2)}} \times \sqrt{\frac{1}{N_1} + \frac{1}{N_2}}} \qquad \text{(Ex. 3–6)}$$

The $t$ will be explained below, but we can see the differences between this formula and that in example 3–3: before taking the square root in the denominator we (1) multiply the square of the two standard deviations by the number of people in the respective samples minus one, (2) instead of dividing by the total number of the two samples, we divide by that number minus two, and (3) we take that result and multiply it by the square root of the sum of each of the two samples divided into one.

If we suppose that in example 3–5, concerning the ages of houses in Chicago and Detroit, only ten houses in Chicago and fifteen in Detroit were involved, but that the means and standard deviations remained the same, we can solve for the significance of the difference between the means.

$$t = \frac{23 - 21}{\sqrt{\frac{(4^2 \times 9) + (5^2 \times 14)}{15 + 10 - 2}} \times \sqrt{\frac{1}{15} + \frac{1}{10}}}$$

$$= \frac{2}{\sqrt{\frac{(16 \times 9) + (25 \times 14)}{23}} \times \sqrt{\frac{5}{30}}}$$

$$= \frac{2}{\sqrt{\frac{144 + 300}{23}} \times \sqrt{\frac{5}{30}}}$$

$$= \frac{2}{\sqrt{21.48} \times \sqrt{.17}}$$

$$= \frac{2}{4.63 \times .41}$$

$$= \frac{2}{1.90}$$

$$= \quad 1.05 \tag{Ex. 3–7}$$

To determine the meaning of the value of $t$, we go to a mathematical table called *t-distribution*, presented here as table 3–1. The numbers on the left of the table, *degrees of freedom*, are calculated by adding the number of the two samples and then subtracting two ($df = N_1 + N_2 - 2$). For the above problem, then, there are twenty-three degrees of freedom ($15 + 10 - 2 = 23$). We see that for our results to be significant at $p < .05$, we must have $t = 2.069$ at least; the conclusion, then, is that given the smaller samples, our results are not significant at $p < .05$, even though they were so when the samples were larger.

A word of caution here may be in order. I am not suggesting that statistical tests be used slavishly and unthinkingly or even that all linguistic data are suitable for statistical testing. In example 3–7, for instance, the difference between the two small sample means was significant at $p < .40$, meaning of course, that there is a 40 percent probability that our results happened by chance. Had it been determined previously that we would accept $p < .40$, then clearly our results would have been significant and acceptable. What is basic, however, is that the researcher state in advance, for himself or herself and later for the reader, the level of significance which he or she is going to use; $p < .05$ is the minimum generally used in the social sciences, so it has been used here as well.

To this point we have been trying to evaluate and interpret the differences between means of frequency distributions. Sometimes, however, data are presented simply in terms of percentages, and no frequency distribution is possible. For example, let us suppose that a public opinion poll sampling opinions concerning the Equal Rights Amendment (ERA) finds that 40 percent of fifty men and 50 percent of sixty women in the sample are in favor of it. Here we cannot set up a frequency distribution, since the answers in each case are either yes or no. How can one determine if the difference in the opinions of the sexes is significant? To do so, we need what we shall call the *proportion test*, and it is calculated in two stages.

The first stage involves using the following formula, which requires multiplying both percentages ($p_1$ and $p_2$) by the number of people in the respective samples, adding those results together, and then dividing by the total number of people sampled. The solution is called *pi* ($\pi$), the sampling error. (The meaning and explanation of sampling error are beyond the scope of this book.)

$$\pi = \frac{N_1 p_1 + N_2 p_2}{N_1 + N_2}$$

(Ex. 3–8)

In our Equal Rights Amendment poll then, $p_1 = .40$, $p_2 = .50$, $N_1 = 50$, and $N_2 = 60$, so that we can fit these numbers into the formula in example 3–9.

$$\pi = \frac{(50 \times .40) + (60 \times .50)}{50 + 60}$$

$$= \frac{20 + 30}{110}$$

$$= .45$$

(Ex. 3–9)

Once pi has been calculated, it can be put into a second formula which will tell us if the results of the poll are significant at $p < .05$. Again, our results must be at least 1.96.

$$z = \frac{p_1 - p_2}{\sqrt{\pi (1 - \pi) \; (1/N_1 + 1/N_2)}}$$

(Ex. 3–10)

Since calculated that $\pi = .45$, and we already know that $p_1 = .40$, $p_2 = .50$, $N_1 = 50$, and $N_2 = 60$, we can solve the formula:

$$z = \frac{.40 - .50}{\sqrt{(.45)(.55) \quad (1/50 + 1/60)}}$$

$$= \frac{.10}{.095}$$

$$= 1.05 \text{ (less than 1.96)}$$

(Ex. 3–11)

We see that the difference between the opinions of the men and the women is not significant at $p < .05$.

*Table 3–1*. *t*-Distribution

| df | .5 | .4 | .3 | .2 |
|----|------|------|------|------|
| 1 | 1.000 | 1.376 | 1.963 | 3.078 |
| 2 | .816 | 1.061 | 1.386 | 1.886 |
| 3 | .765 | .978 | 1.250 | 1.638 |
| 4 | .741 | .941 | 1.190 | 1.533 |
| 5 | .727 | .920 | 1.156 | 1.476 |
| 6 | .718 | .906 | 1.134 | 1.440 |
| 7 | .711 | .896 | 1.119 | 1.415 |
| 8 | .706 | .889 | 1.108 | 1.397 |
| 9 | .703 | .883 | 1.100 | 1.383 |
| 10 | .700 | .879 | 1.093 | 1.372 |
| 11 | .697 | .876 | 1.088 | 1.363 |
| 12 | .695 | .873 | 1.083 | 1.356 |
| 13 | .694 | .870 | 1.079 | 1.350 |
| 14 | .692 | .868 | 1.076 | 1.345 |
| 15 | .691 | .866 | 1.074 | 1.341 |
| 16 | .690 | .865 | 1.071 | 1.337 |
| 17 | .689 | .863 | 1.069 | 1.333 |
| 18 | .688 | .862 | 1.067 | 1.330 |
| 19 | .688 | .861 | 1.066 | 1.328 |
| 20 | .687 | .860 | 1.064 | 1.325 |
| 21 | .686 | .859 | 1.063 | 1.323 |
| 22 | .686 | .858 | 1.061 | 1.321 |
| 23 | .685 | .858 | 1.060 | 1.319 |
| 24 | .685 | .857 | 1.059 | 1.318 |
| 25 | .684 | .856 | 1.058 | 1.316 |
| 26 | .684 | .856 | 1.058 | 1.315 |
| 27 | .684 | .855 | 1.057 | 1.314 |
| 28 | .683 | .855 | 1.056 | 1.313 |
| 29 | .683 | .854 | 1.055 | 1.311 |
| 30 | .683 | .854 | 1.055 | 1.310 |
| ∞ | .67449 | .84162 | 1.03643 | 1.28155 |

*Source*: Abridged from Fisher 1970:176.

| .1 | .05 | .02 | .01 |
|---|---|---|---|
| 6.314 | 12.706 | 31.821 | 63.657 |
| 2.920 | 4.303 | 6.965 | 9.925 |
| 2.353 | 3.182 | 4.541 | 5.841 |
| 2.132 | 2.776 | 3.747 | 4.604 |
| 2.015 | 2.571 | 3.365 | 4.032 |
| 1.943 | 2.447 | 3.143 | 3.707 |
| 1.895 | 2.365 | 2.998 | 3.499 |
| 1.860 | 2.306 | 2.896 | 3.355 |
| 1.833 | 2.262 | 2.821 | 3.250 |
| 1.812 | 2.228 | 2.764 | 3.169 |
| 1.796 | 2.201 | 2.718 | 3.106 |
| 1.782 | 2.179 | 2.681 | 3.055 |
| 1.771 | 2.160 | 2.650 | 3.012 |
| 1.761 | 2.145 | 2.624 | 2.977 |
| 1.753 | 2.131 | 2.602 | 2.947 |
| 1.746 | 2.120 | 2.583 | 2.921 |
| 1.740 | 2.110 | 2.567 | 2.898 |
| 1.734 | 2.101 | 2.552 | 2.878 |
| 1.729 | 2.093 | 2.539 | 2.861 |
| 1.725 | 2.086 | 2.528 | 2.845 |
| 1.721 | 2.080 | 2.518 | 2.831 |
| 1.717 | 2.074 | 2.508 | 2.819 |
| 1.714 | 2.069 | 2.500 | 2.807 |
| 1.711 | 2.064 | 2.492 | 2.797 |
| 1.708 | 2.060 | 2.485 | 2.787 |
| 1.706 | 2.056 | 2.479 | 2.779 |
| 1.703 | 2.052 | 2.473 | 2.771 |
| 1.701 | 2.048 | 2.467 | 2.763 |
| 1.699 | 2.045 | 2.462 | 2.756 |
| 1.697 | 2.042 | 2.457 | 2.750 |
| 1.64485 | 1.95996 | 2.32634 | 2.57582 |

Another poll finds that 50 percent of 300 men and 60 percent of 200 women favor ERA. Is this poll significant at $p < .05$? To find out, we first solve for pi, remembering that now $p_1 = .50$, $p_2 = .60$, $N_1 = 300$, and $N_2 = 200$.

$$\pi = \frac{(300 \times .50) + (200 \times .60)}{300 + 200}$$

$$= \frac{150 + 120}{500}$$

$$= .54 \qquad\qquad\qquad (\text{Ex. } 3\text{--}12)$$

Now that pi has been determined, we can solve for $z$:

$$z = \frac{p_1 - p_2}{\sqrt{\pi (1 - \pi)} \quad (1/N_1 + 1/N_2)}$$

$$= \frac{.10}{\sqrt{(.54) \quad (.46)} \quad (1/300 + 1/200)}$$

$$= \frac{.10}{\sqrt{.0021}}$$

$$= \frac{.10}{.0458}$$

$$= 2.183 \qquad\qquad\qquad (\text{Ex. } 3\text{--}13)$$

Since the solution (2.183) is greater than 1.96, the results of the second poll are indeed significant at $p < .05$ but not at $p < .01$ (we would need a $z$ of at least 2.58).

This proportion test is good only if two percentages are to be compared. If there are more than two, we use what is perhaps the best known of all tests in statistics: *chi-square* ($\chi^2$). For example, if we wanted to compare 100 students taking both math and English, their grades (in this case C or above) could be arranged in a table such as table 3–2. It

*Table 3–2*. Chi-Square Table for Grades in English and Math

| Math | English | | | Total |
|---|---|---|---|---|
| | A | B | C | |
| A | 10 | 11 | 9 | 30 |
| B | 7 | 5 | 20 | 32 |
| C | 16 | 13 | 9 | 38 |
| Total | 33 | 29 | 38 | 100 |

should be obvious that just by looking at table 3–2, one cannot tell whether there is a relationship between grades in English and grades in math. We need to calculate chi-square to find out, and the first thing to do is to calculate what we would expect the numbers in table 3–2 to be if there were *no* relationship at all. To do this, we note that 30 percent got an A in math, 32 percent got a B in math, and 38 percent got a C. Then we multiply the totals of the vertical columns by these percentages (see table 3–3). These "expected" responses can then be combined with the actual responses. In table 3–4 the expected responses are in parentheses. Now we use the following formula for chi-square.

$$\chi^2 = \Sigma \; \frac{(\text{actual} - \text{expected})^2}{\text{expected}} \qquad \text{(Ex. 3–14)}$$

That is, we subtract the expected responses from the actual responses, square the result, divide by the expected number, and add up the results for each box in table 3–4.

*Table 3–3*. Chi-Square Calculations, Expected Scores in English and Math

| Math | English | | |
|---|---|---|---|
| | A | B | C |
| A | 33 × .30 = 9.90 | 29 × .30 = 8.70 | 38 × .30 = 11.40 |
| B | 33 × .32 = 10.56 | 29 × .32 = 9.28 | 38 × .32 = 12.16 |
| C | 33 × .38 = 12.54 | 29 × .38 = 11.02 | 38 × .38 = 14.44 |

*Table 3–4.* Chi-Square Calculations, Actual and Expected Grades in English and Math

|        | English |  |  |
|--------|---------|---------|---------|
| Math   | A       | B       | C       |
| A      | 10 (9.90) | 11 (8.70) | 9 (11.40) |
| B      | 7 (10.56) | 5 (9.28) | 20 (12.16) |
| C      | 16 (12.54) | 13 (11.02) | 9 (14.44) |

*Note:* Grades in parentheses are expected.

$$\chi^2 = \frac{(10 - 9.90)^2}{9.90} + \frac{(11 - 8.70)^2}{8.70} + \frac{(9 - 11.40)^2}{11.40}$$

$$+ \frac{(7 - 10.56)^2}{10.56} + \frac{(5 - 9.28)^2}{9.28} + \frac{(20 - 12.96)^2}{12.96}$$

$$+ \frac{(16 - 12.54)^2}{12.54} + \frac{(13 - 11.02)^2}{11.02} + \frac{(9 - 14.44)^2}{14.44}$$

$$= .001 + 1.20 + .95 + .61 + 1.97 + .32 + .50 + 5.05 + 2.05$$

$$= 12.65 \hspace{4cm} \text{(Ex. 3–15)}$$

Now, as with the *t*-test, we must calculate the number of degrees of freedom. For chi-square we use the following formula: $df = (r - 1)(c - 1)$, where $r$ is the number of horizontal rows and $c$ is the number of vertical columns. In this case, $df = (3 - 1)(3 - 1) = 2 \times 2 = 4$. Now we go to a chi-square table such as that in table 3–5, which can be found in almost any statistics book. At four degrees of freedom, table 3.5 indicates that when $p < .05$, $\chi^2 = 9.488$, whereas by our calculation $\chi^2 = 12.65$; so our results are clearly significant at $p < .05$. A second look at the table reveals that the relationship between grades in English and in math is significant even at $p < .02$, meaning that there are only 2 chances in 100 that the results in table 3–2 could have happened by chance. In other words, we calculated that $\chi^2 = 12.65$, larger than 11.668 ($p < .02$, $df = 4$).

One final point must be made about chi-square. It is not generally valid if the number of expected responses in any one box in a table such as table 3–4 is three or fewer. Moreover, the chi-square test is designed to be used on large samples; that is, on samples no smaller than thirty.

*Table 3–5.* Values of Chi-Square

| df | .50 | .30 | .20 | .10 | .05 | .02 | .01 |
|----|-----|-----|-----|-----|-----|-----|-----|
| 1 | .455 | 1.074 | 1.642 | 2.706 | 3.841 | 5.412 | 6.635 |
| 2 | 1.386 | 2.408 | 3.219 | 4.605 | 5.991 | 7.824 | 9.210 |
| 3 | 2.366 | 3.665 | 4.642 | 6.251 | 7.815 | 9.837 | 11.345 |
| 4 | 3.357 | 4.878 | 5.989 | 7.779 | 9.488 | 11.668 | 13.277 |
| 5 | 4.351 | 6.064 | 7.289 | 9.236 | 11.070 | 13.388 | 15.086 |
| 6 | 5.348 | 7.231 | 8.558 | 10.645 | 12.592 | 15.033 | 16.812 |
| 7 | 6.346 | 8.383 | 9.803 | 12.017 | 14.067 | 16.622 | 18.475 |
| 8 | 7.344 | 9.524 | 11.030 | 13.362 | 15.507 | 18.168 | 20.090 |
| 9 | 8.343 | 10.656 | 12.242 | 14.684 | 16.919 | 19.679 | 21.666 |
| 10 | 9.342 | 11.781 | 13.442 | 15.987 | 18.307 | 21.161 | 23.209 |
| 11 | 10.341 | 12.899 | 14.631 | 17.275 | 19.675 | 22.618 | 24.725 |
| 12 | 11.340 | 14.011 | 15.812 | 18.549 | 21.026 | 24.054 | 26.217 |
| 13 | 12.340 | 15.119 | 16.985 | 19.812 | 22.362 | 25.472 | 27.688 |
| 14 | 13.339 | 16.222 | 18.151 | 21.064 | 23.685 | 26.873 | 29.141 |
| 15 | 14.339 | 17.322 | 19.311 | 22.307 | 24.996 | 28.259 | 30.578 |
| 16 | 15.338 | 18.418 | 20.465 | 23.542 | 26.296 | 29.633 | 32.000 |
| 17 | 16.338 | 19.511 | 21.615 | 24.769 | 27.587 | 30.995 | 33.409 |
| 18 | 17.338 | 20.601 | 22.760 | 25.989 | 28.869 | 32.346 | 34.805 |
| 19 | 18.338 | 21.689 | 23.900 | 27.204 | 30.144 | 33.687 | 36.191 |
| 20 | 19.337 | 22.775 | 25.038 | 28.412 | 31.410 | 35.020 | 37.566 |
| 21 | 20.337 | 23.858 | 26.171 | 29.615 | 32.671 | 36.343 | 38.932 |
| 22 | 21.337 | 24.939 | 27.301 | 30.813 | 33.924 | 37.659 | 40.289 |
| 23 | 22.337 | 26.018 | 28.429 | 32.007 | 35.172 | 38.968 | 41.638 |
| 24 | 23.337 | 27.096 | 29.553 | 33.196 | 36.415 | 40.270 | 42.980 |
| 25 | 24.337 | 28.172 | 30.675 | 34.382 | 37.652 | 41.566 | 44.314 |
| 26 | 25.336 | 29.246 | 31.795 | 35.563 | 38.885 | 42.856 | 45.642 |
| 27 | 26.336 | 30.319 | 32.912 | 36.741 | 40.113 | 44.140 | 46.963 |
| 28 | 27.336 | 31.391 | 34.027 | 37.916 | 41.337 | 45.419 | 48.278 |
| 29 | 28.336 | 32.461 | 35.139 | 39.087 | 42.557 | 46.693 | 49.588 |
| 30 | 29.336 | 33.530 | 36.250 | 40.256 | 43.773 | 47.962 | 50.892 |

It should be clear by now that we cannot evaluate and interpret the results of a quantitative analysis of data without using statistical tests. Just looking at the results is not sufficient, mainly because too many factors are involved. In comparing two means, one must take into account standard deviation and sample size as well. In evaluating two proportions or percentages, sample size is vital. And only a person very experienced in statistical analysis could know simply by looking at the results in table 3–2 that there are only 2 chances in 100 that those results are not related. Results, in other words, are never simply "obvious"; they are significant at various levels of significance, and those levels should be calculated by the researcher.

The statistical tests presented in this chapter are, for the most part, presented without much explanation as to why they work. We noted that they are based on the theory of probabilities, but we did not enter into the question of how the formulas are derived. Instead, we looked at them in much the same way that we would look at a cookbook. For our purposes we need only determine which test to use, find the appropriate formula, and add our "ingredients": the numbers required by the formula. In some cases the definitions of symbols used in the classical formulation of the tests in statistics books have been simplified here. They may be important to statisticians, but not to most linguists and certainly not to the reader for whom this book is intended. The important thing is to know which tests to use and how to calculate them.

The tests provided in this section should be sufficient for our purposes: to permit us to evaluate recent work in social dialectology. A look at any statistics book shows that there are many more tests, but many of them are not especially relevant for the evaluation of linguistic data. The examples in this section have been nonlinguistic, and my choice was purposeful—to give a general idea as to how data can be evaluated and interpreted using the tools of statistics. We will apply these tests to language data in the later sections of this chapter.

As we shall see, most of the results of studies in social dialectology are presented in terms of percentages, and some of the authors of these studies do not test the significance of their data. Instead, they let their charts and tables speak for themselves. In some cases, we ourselves will be able to perform the appropriate statistical tests, so that we will have the opportunity to evaluate better the results of the various studies.

## Social Dialectology: The First Stages

We noted earlier that social dialectology in its most basic sense is the study of the relationship between language variety, or dialect, and social class. The idea that there is an intimate relationship between social structure and language structure is not a new one; it goes back at least as far as Wilhelm von Humboldt's *Essai sur les langues du nouveau continent* (1820–1822). The notion of the close connection between language and society was best stated, however, by the French linguist Antoine Meillet (1906:17) in a lecture he delivered on February 13, 1906, which I have translated:

> . . . it is an *a priori* possibility that any modification of social structure will have as a repercussion a change in the conditions in which language de-

velops. . . . but by the very fact that language is a social institution, it follows that linguistics is a social science, and that the only variable one might invoke to account for linguistic change is social change, of which language changes are only consequences, sometimes immediate and direct, but most often mediated and indirect.

And yet, in spite of this and other, similar statements about the inter-relationship between linguistics and the other social sciences, very little actual research was carried out in this area during the first half of the twentieth century. The linguistic theories of Bloomfield (1933), and later of Chomsky (1965), in fact tended to treat language as something apart from society, as a patient to be placed upon the operating table and dissected without much reference, if any, to the culture in which the language lived. On the other hand, the three informant types inter-viewed for the American atlas projects did provide an obvious starting point for work on social dialects, so it is not particularly surprising that the first research in the field was conducted using American field records.

Although a number of scholars throughout the centuries had written about the social implications of language use, Raven I. McDavid, Jr., in 1948, published the first article which approached linguistic problems from a strictly sociolinguistic point of view. McDavid examined the atlas data from South Carolina but found no significant geographical pattern for the presence or absence of the constriction of postvocalic /r/. Post-vocalic /r/ constriction in words such as *worm, father, barn, beard,* and so forth, when examined in the context of regional dialectology, seemed basically chaotic and haphazard, even when McDavid took settlement history into account. The area where /r/ was originally pronounced was quite small.

A social analysis, however, revealed anything but chaos. It revealed that the spread of the loss of constriction of postvocalic /r/ generally paralleled the spread inland of the plantation culture from Charleston. The upper class of Charleston, even in early colonial times, always iden-tified with things English. Whereas upper-class New Englanders sent their sons to Harvard, the upper class in Charleston sent their sons to Oxford and Cambridge. Similarly, upper-class Charlestonians tended to imitate London English. When we add this information to the fact that the Charleston upper class has always had a high social standing every-where in South Carolina, the spread of the loss of constriction of post-vocalic /r/ becomes more easily explainable: "In any event, the prestige of the old plantation caste has meant the spread inland of their speech ways, including the lack of constriction of postvocalic -*r*, and the trend toward the loss of constriction continues" (McDavid 1948:203).

After McDavid's pioneering work, several other studies followed, all based on American field records. In the last chapter we noted that *The Pronunciation of English in the Atlantic States* by Kurath and McDavid was devoted in a large measure to identifying differences in cultivated speech. Similarly, Atwood's *Survey of Verb Forms in the Eastern United States* was in many ways a sociolinguistic study and not simple dialect geography. Note Atwood's (1953) description of his findings for the past forms of *bring*:

Bring (27)

The past participle is recorded in the context "I have (brought) your coat."

*Brought* /brɔt/ is very heavily dominant in all major areas among all classes.

*Brung* /brʌŋ/ occurs in a very scattered fashion throughout the Eastern States. There are 51 occurrences divided among New England, New York, New Jersey, Pennsylvania, Ohio, West Virginia, North Carolina, South Carolina, and Georgia. . . . It is dominantly a Type I form, but in Pennsylvania and West Virginia almost as many Type II informants use it.

One New England informant used *broughten* /brɔtən/ and a few southern Negroes say *done bring*. [P. 7]

This quite admirable blend of regional and social dialectology was typical of the kind of work done by those scholars affiliated in one way or another with American atlas projects. And their students carried on in the same tradition: Lee A. Pederson, the director of the *Linguistic Atlas of the Gulf States*, wrote his doctoral dissertation, "The Pronunciation of English in Metropolitan Chicago," under the tutelage of McDavid at the University of Chicago and modified the atlas worksheets for that urban situation.

During this same time, we must remember, the atlas methods were attacked by Glenna Pickford, and it was only natural for those scholars interested in social variation in language to attempt to change some of their methods in order to meet such objections. The change, when it came, was quite sudden—the publication of *The Social Stratification of English in New York City*, the doctoral dissertation of William Labov (1966). Labov, a linguist not in the atlas tradition at all, had a profound effect on the study of social variation in language; so much so, in fact, that it would not be an exaggeration to suggest that the changes wrought by Labov's work were truly revolutionary. For this reason, we would do well to examine Labov's methods and results in some detail.

## The Social Stratification of English in New York City

Labov began his study with a critique of previous work on New York City speech. He noted that the criteria for atlas informants mean that atlas studies in the major cities do not sample large and important segments of the populations of those cities, populations which in fact influence dialect patterns. In his atlas-type study of the speech of New York City, for example, Allen F. Hubbell (1950) did not interview any informants representing the groups who had come there in large numbers during the past eighty years: blacks, Italians, Jews, and Puerto Ricans.

In the early 1960s, in spite of the fact that Hubbell and others had argued that the pronunciation of postvocalic /r/ was essentially haphazard, Labov found that there are social determinants of the use of postvocalic /r/. In one of the most fascinating studies conducted in social dialectology, Labov, like McDavid before him, was able to show that seemingly haphazard linguistic behavior, when viewed from a sociolinguistic perspective, is part of a well-ordered system.

Labov went to three department stores in New York City—Klein's, Macy's, and Saks Fifth Avenue—and sampled the amount of constriction of postvocalic /r/ in the speech of the employees of the stores. The choice of places was not a random one. Each store caters to a somewhat different range of socioeconomic classes. Klein's services mainly the lower and working classes; Macy's caters to the middle class; Saks Fifth Avenue, with its designer fashions, is visited mainly by the upper middle and the upper classes.

Labov's questionnaire was undoubtedly the shortest in history. He was, in every case, trying to elicit the response *fourth floor*, both in casual and in careful speech. Consequently, one of his interviews might have gone something like this:

Fieldworker: "Where can I find ladies' dresses?"
Informant: "Fourth floor."
Fieldworker: "What did you say?"
Informant: "Fourth floor!!"

Labov quite rightly reasoned that the informant would be somewhat more careful in the second response, and he was hence able to record the informants' behavior in essentially two different linguistic styles. The results, far from demonstrating that New Yorkers pronounce postvocalic /r/ haphazardly, showed that there is clear class differentiation. In figure 3–1 the shaded areas show the percentage of cases of informants

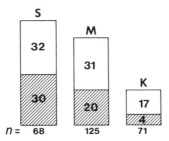

*Figure 3–1.* Overall Stratification of (r) by Store. S = Saks, M = Macy's, K = Klein's. Shaded area = % *all (r-1)*; unshaded area = % *some (r-1)*. *Source*: Labov 1966:73.

who used constricted postvocalic /r/ in all four possible places where it could be pronounced, and the white areas show the percentage of people who constricted postvocalic /r/ at least once. Labov's term for postvocalic /r/ constriction is (r–1). Figure 3–1 indicates that there is a clear social class stratification for postvocalic /r/ in the three stores. Furthermore, Labov was able to show, he said, that as the informants were asked to repeat the utterance *fourth floor*, the percentage of the constriction of postvocalic /r/ also increased. Figure 3–2 presents Labov's results, in percentages, for the amount of constriction of postvocalic /r/ in all four positions for both the first and the second occurrences of the utterance *fourth floor*. Labov does not evaluate the reliability of these data, but figures 3–1 and 3–2 do indeed look convincing. We shall return to them later in this chapter.

After this admittedly preliminary study, Labov set out to sample in a more scientific fashion the social stratification of both postvocalic /r/ and other variables as well for the whole of New York City. Like all good

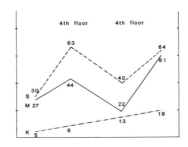

*Figure 3–2.* Percentage Constriction of Postvocalic /r/ at Three Stores. S = Saks, M = Macy's, K = Klein's. *Source*: Labov 1966:74.

scientists, Labov first looked at previous research on New York City speech and thus found four other variables in addition to /r/: the vowel in words such as *bad, bag, ask*; the vowel in *dog, coffee, caught,* and so forth; the first sound in words such as *thin, three,* and *thought*; and the first sound in words such as *they, there,* and *then.*

Labov also refined considerably the two styles which he had used in the original department store study, although he did maintain the general distinction between careful and casual speech. Careful speech, however, was subdivided into four different categories:

1. Context B: the interview situation. This is essentially the style one finds in all atlas-type interviewing, including the fieldwork of the *LANE* or the *SED.*
2. Context C: reading of a selected passage of prose.
3. Context D: reading of word lists.
4. Context D': reading of minimal pairs such as *den/then.*

Of these four styles, increasing from B to D' in the degree of care exercised by the informant, only C requires some explanation here. For context C, the passages to be read contained a large number of the variable under consideration. The following example from Labov's questionnaire contains six instances of postvocalic /r/ and three of one of the *th*-sounds /ð/: "You're certainly in *the* dark! *They* tore down *that* dock ten years ago, when you were in diapers."

Labov also provides five different contexts which he calls casual in nature:

A–1: speech outside the formal interview
A–2: conversation with a third person
A–3: response to questions
A–4: childhood rhymes
A–5: danger of death

Each of the above requires some brief explanation except A–3. A–1 is the style when, during the course of the interview (context B), the informant might ask the fieldworker, "Do you want a beer?" Such a question obviously provides the fieldworker with an opportunity to record a pronunciation of postvocalic /r/. A–2 occurs when the informant stops the process of the interview in order to speak, for example, to a member of his family: "Johnny, get away from *there*!" A–4 is when the informant is asked specifically to repeat childhood rhymes. Labov gives the following as one example:

Glory, glory, Hallelujah
The teacher hit me with a ruler.
The ruler turned red
And the teacher dropped dead.
No more school for me.

Clearly, such a rhyme provides evidence for the constriction of postvocalic /r/, since if the informant uses constricted postvocalic /r/, the little
poem does not rhyme.

The final context, A–5, according to Labov, is the most casual one
which can be elicited during a linguistic interview. The fieldworker asks
the informant if he was ever in a situation where he was in danger of
dying. If the informant does answer affirmatively, the fieldworker asks
to hear what happened. In this situation, the informant will be anxious
to impress the fieldworker with the seriousness of the situation and,
according to Labov, the informant will be less on guard linguistically.

For each of these nine *contextual styles*, as Labov calls them, the
fieldworker must also look for clues as to the psychological state of the
informant. Labov argues that there are four *channel cues* which can help
determine the emotional state of an informant and can hence indicate
the amount of care the informant is taking during his interview. These
channel cues are tempo, pitch, volume, and breathing. Obviously, if an
informant starts to speak more rapidly and more loudly, raises the pitch
of his voice, and starts to breathe somewhat more heavily, he is more
excited and consequently less on his guard linguistically.

Not only were Labov's methods and goals of interviewing different
from those of linguistic atlas-type studies, but his criteria for informant
selection also differed markedly from those of earlier studies. We noted,
for example, that given the criteria for atlas informants, Hubbell's 1950
study did not sample the speech of groups such as Italians, blacks, Jews,
or Puerto Ricans. With some minor exceptions, Labov chose informants
who had lived in New York City all their lives, but he did not, as had atlas
fieldworkers, look for the oldest living descendants of the oldest families.
Such people are too much in the minority to be clearly representative of
the speech of the city.

We noted that Glenna Pickford attacked the *LANE* for not using a
random sample, for not allowing each member of the total population of
New England a chance at being selected. Labov, in fact, attempted to
follow Pickford's suggestion and used a random sample which had been
previously selected for a sociological survey. The original sample had
been made by Mobilization for Youth and contained 1,000 informants.
For various reasons, including the fact that many of the Mobilization for
Youth informants were Puerto Rican and hence were not native speak-

ers of English, Labov was forced to reduce the sample size. When he finished cutting, he had a total of eighty-eight native speakers of English who fitted all of his criteria. Pickford had argued that the *LANE* sample was biased because it sampled only those informants who were willing to be interviewed; Labov, however, added a "television interview." If one of the people selected to be an informant did refuse to talk to the field-worker, the fieldworker telephoned him and asked questions about the television program the informant was watching. In this way, Labov was able to obtain at least some information even from those who had refused the more straightforward approach.

Labov's typing of informants into classes was far more sophisticated than that of the atlas projects; he used three criteria: education, occupation, and income. All three of these data were easily accessible from the Mobilization for Youth files, and Labov set up ten different social classes for New York City. The digit 0 denoted lower class and 9 was upper middle class, the highest class in Labov's study. Table 3–6 gives some indication of the criteria used by Labov to set up his classes.

One of the tasks of the New York City language study, then, was to see if the trends noted in the early department store survey were truly valid. To what extent, if any, can one correlate linguistic variation with (1) contextual style and (2) socioeconomic class? The results were extremely clear in a number of cases and showed that there is indeed a correlation between linguistic behavior and social class and that within the classes there is a correlation between language variety and contextual style. As far as the latter is concerned, we can return to the question of postvocalic /r/ and take a look at the results for two informants in the various styles already explained. In both cases, all the casual styles (A–1 through A–5) are listed together. The first case is that of "Miss Josephine P.," of Italian extraction and a receptionist at Saks Fifth Avenue. The numbers represent the percentage of constricted postvocalic /r/ in the informant's speech at the various stylistic levels:

|       | A  | B  | C  | D  | D' |
|-------|----|----|----|----|----|
| (r–1) | 00 | 03 | 23 | 53 | 50 |

As we can see, there is a general progression toward more use of constricted postvocalic /-r/ as the situation becomes more formal and the informant pays more attention to the kind of language she is using. Similarly, with "Abraham G.," a high school graduate, we get the following results:

|       | A  | B  | C  | D   | D'  |
|-------|----|----|----|-----|-----|
| (r–1) | 12 | 15 | 46 | 100 | 100 |

*Table 3–6.* The Distribution of the Population and Their Educational, Occupational, and Income Characteristics

| Class | Education | Characteristic | | % of the national population |
|---|---|---|---|---|
| | | Occupation | Income | |
| Not in Labov's study | | | | |
| V. Upper class | College graduate of the *right* school | First-rate professional, manager, official, or proprietor of a large business | Don't bother to count it | 1 |
| Labov class 9 | | | | |
| IV. Upper middle class | College graduate | Careermen in professions, managerial, official, or large business positions | Equally high but they count it | 9 |

| | Education | Occupation | Income | % |
|---|---|---|---|---|
| **Labov's classes 6–8**<br>III. Lower middle class | High school graduate, frequently with specialized training thereafter | Semiprofessionals, petty businessmen, white collar, foremen, and craftsmen | Enough to save for children's college education | 40 |
| **Labov's classes 1–5**<br>II. Working class | Some high school | Operatives: blue-collar workers at the mercy of the labor market | Enough for cars, TV, etc. | 40 |
| **Labov's class 0**<br>I. Lower class | Grade school or less | Laborers: last to be hired and first to be fired; frequent job shifts | Struggle for bare existence | 10 |

*Note*: Kahl's social class divisions are indicated by Roman numerals.
*Source*: Labov 1966:217.

The results for the correlation between the use of the five variables and social class were, in the main, also quite neat, as figure 3–3 indicates. The symbol (th) here indicates the pronunciation [t] instead of the standard [θ] as the first sound in words such as *thin*, and (dh) is Labov's designation for the pronunciation [d] instead of the standard [ð] in words such as *then*. In all social classes, the language of the informants becomes more standard as the situation becomes more formal, but the higher classes generally use more standard forms than do the others in every contextual style.

Labov's questionnaire also contained what he called a "subjective reaction test"; that is, he asked people to react to taped samples of speech containing the five variables used for the study. The results were interesting. For example, he discovered that the very people who use nonstandard forms the most are the first to condemn their use in the speech of others. In other words, we often are unaware of our own linguistic behavior. Linguistic atlas fieldworkers had known this for a long time, but Labov was able to use this fact and organize it into a linguistic model.

Perhaps the most important contribution of Labov's study is the notion that linguistic behavior is inconsistent but that the inconsistency is, paradoxically, ordered. What to earlier investigators of New York City speech appeared to be haphazard use of constricted postvocalic /r/, for example, was not so. But one has to count the occurrences of the variable before the systematic behavior can be discovered. As we shall see later in this chapter, just about every sociolinguistic study since Labov has employed the use of linguistic variables and has counted their occurrence. The introduction of quantitative methods, though used to some extent by Atwood in his *Verb Forms*, must be credited to Labov, and in this sense, the changes he wrought for future studies have been truly remarkable.

Certainly all of Labov's results are not as neat as those presented here. In fact, there are several charts in *The Social Stratification of English in New York City* which require considerable explanation and analysis by the author. In such cases, however, Labov is generally able to explain and solve problems by examining the sociolinguistic situation in New York City. Such details are beyond the range of this book. My description of Labov's study, then, has been simplified, with an emphasis on aspects of his work which influenced future research into urban dialects, on the one hand, and the whole of social dialectology, on the other.

## Some Criticisms of Labov's Work

In spite of the fact that many dialectologists hailed the appearance of Labov's study as a considerable step forward in the understanding of

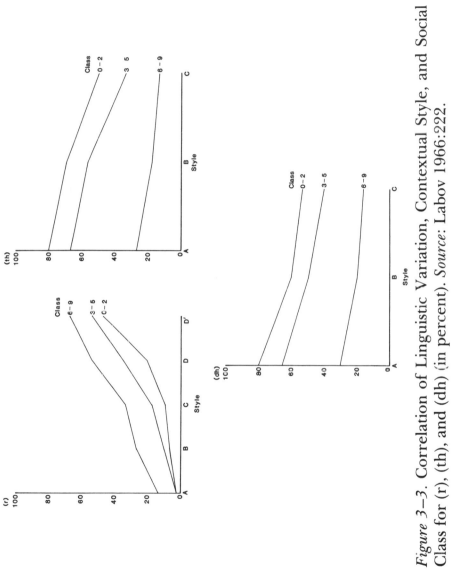

*Figure 3–3.* Correlation of Linguistic Variation, Contextual Style, and Social Class for (r), (th), and (dh) (in percent). *Source:* Labov 1966:222.

urban speech, the response was not uniformly positive. Hans Kurath (1968) criticized Labov for "unwarranted sweeping generalizations" about the nature of linguistic variation in New York City, and Kurath's critique is worth quoting here at some length:

> This [Labov's study] is an ingenious investigation of complicated diffusional changes in pronunciation within a circumscribed area—the Lower East Side of Manhattan (extending from 14th Street to Brooklyn Bridge). . . . However, the correlations of the linguistic variants with special parameters, social types, age groups, and "styles" of speaking presented by Labov in a series of graphs are so smooth and neat that they arouse one's skepticism.
>
> That other parts of New York City—which includes the five boroughs of Manhattan, the Bronx, Staten Island, Brooklyn, and Queens, with a population of 8 million in an area of 320 square miles—conform to the Lower East Side of Manhattan, as Labov maintains, is more than doubtful. Can it be that Washington Heights and Harlem actually agree with the Lower East Side of Manhattan despite fundamental differences in social structure? [P. 6]

Kurath's criticisms here are interesting in that he raises a question about Labov's results because many of them are so very neat. Kurath never tells us why he is suspicious, but certainly neat results of and by themselves do not necessarily have to be suspect. Kurath's second criticism is more valid, in that nowhere in Labov's study does he demonstrate that his results for the Lower East Side are equally true for the rest of the city. Labov notes in his first chapter that in many ways this area represents a microcosm of the speech of New York City as a whole: "The area of New York City that was chosen for intensive study—the Lower East Side—does not represent a simplification of the problem [of describing New York City speech]. On the contrary, it is an area which exemplifies the complexity of New York City as a whole with all its variability and apparent inconsistencies" (Labov 1966:4–5). In the discussion of sampling, however, we noted that one cannot make claims about a population from which no sample has been taken, and we cannot assume automatically that Labov's results are valid for the rest of the city. Although Labov's arguments that the speech of the Lower East Side represents the speech of the whole city are compelling, objectivity nonetheless demands that we reserve judgment about that claim until further research either supports or disproves it.

Another problem with Labov's study involves the fact that he never tests the reliability of his results. Instead, as we noted earlier, he presents his graphs and tables and lets them speak for themselves. A look at the department store survey, however, suggests how this approach can lead to difficulties. Labov notes that the differences in the amount of post-vocalic /r/ constriction in the three stores show a class stratification of that variable, but testing the results shows that they are somewhat less clear.

For example, if we compare Macy's and Klein's in figure 3–2 regarding the pronunciation of *fourth* in what Labov calls the emphatic style, we see that 13 percent of informants exhibited at least some postvocalic /r/ constriction at Klein's; for Macy's, the figure is 22 percent. When we apply the proportion test on these data, however, we find that they are not significant at $p < .05$; in fact, they are not reliable even at $p < .20$, so there is a better than 20 percent probability that the results are a function of chance alone, of the specific sample that Labov chose.

On the other hand, the proportion test reveals that, at the casual style, the difference between the levels of postvocalic /r/ at Saks and Macy's is indeed valid at $p < .05$ ($z = 2.21$) for the pronunciation of *floor*. What is important here, however, is not the above tests on the data (many more could be performed) but rather the fact that nowhere in his classic study of New York City English does Labov subject his results to rigorous testing. If he had done so on the department store findings, his conclusions in some cases would have been strengthened; in other cases, quite the opposite would have happened, but one can be certain that the analysis would have been somewhat different.

In every case, the differences between Saks Fifth Avenue and Klein's are significant at $p < .05$, and except for the instance of *fourth* (emphatic), the Macy's and Klein's results are also significant at $p < .05$. On the other hand, the data for style levels are far less convincing. If we use the proportion test and compare the two pronunciations of both *fourth* and *floor*, we see that, for Saks, the difference for *fourth* of 10 percent is not significant at $p < .05$; $z = 1.04$, so the results are reliable only at about $p < .30$. In fact, the only style difference for any of the three stores which is reliable at $p < .05$ is the instance of *floor* at Macy's. None of the other differences comes anywhere close to $p < .05$. Both of the style shifts for Klein's are valid well above $p < .05$ and are thus above the minimum confidence level acceptable in the social sciences. Nevertheless, these data form the basis for the following claim: "The fact that the figures for (r–1) [constricted postvocalic /r/] at Klein's are low should not obscure the fact that Klein's employees also participate in the same pattern of stylistic variation of (r) as the other stores" (Labov 1966:75). This stylistic variation, however, is much less clear once the data have been subjected to tests for reliability.

It must be remembered, however, that the department store survey was never intended to be anything but preliminary, and Labov himself suggests that there are several sources of error in that study. For that reason, we would do well to examine the findings for postvocalic /r/

where Labov included more social classes and all five of the contextual styles. These results are presented in table 3–7 in percentages. *N* refers to the actual numbers of postvocalic /r/ which were counted. The three classes correspond, according to Labov, to lower (0–2), working (3–5), and middle (6–9).

Although Labov does not test the reliability of these results, he does give enough information to permit the proportion test. A comparison of the lowest and highest classes (0–2 and 6–9, respectively), reveals that that differences between them for styles A, B, and D are significant at $p < .01$ or better. The difference for style C is significant at $p < .05$, but for style D', $z = 1.82$, below the required 1.96. Still, the tests reveal that Labov's general claims are valid regarding class stratification of the variable.

This validity, however, holds only up to a point. For example, if we compare the upper two classes, we find that the differences for styles A and B are valid at $p < .01$ and that the differences for style D are valid at $p < .05$. Neither style C nor style D' shows significant class differences at $p < .05$. Similarly, a comparison of the lower two classes reveals that the

*Table 3–7.* Class Stratification of Labov's (1966) Variables

|  | | Style | | | | | | *N* | | |
|---|---|---|---|---|---|---|---|---|---|---|
|  | A | B | C | D | D' | A | B | C | D | D' |
| Class group 0–2 | | | | | | | | | | |
| (r) | .25 | 10.5 | 14.5 | 23.5 | 49.5 | 18 | 22 | 14 | 17 | 17 |
| (eh) | 23.0 | 27.0 | 29.0 | 32.0 | | 13 | 21 | 13 | 17 | |
| (oh) | 23.0 | 24.0 | 24.0 | 21.0 | | 16 | 22 | 13 | 15 | |
| (th) | 78.0 | 65.0 | 43.5 | | | 18 | 22 | 13 | | |
| (dh) | 78.5 | 56.0 | 49.0 | | | 17 | 22 | 13 | | |
| Class group 3–5 | | | | | | | | | | |
| (r) | 4.0 | 12.5 | 21.0 | 35.0 | 55.0 | 26 | 28 | 26 | 27 | 26 |
| (eh) | 25.0 | 28.0 | 30.5 | 32.0 | | 21 | 27 | 26 | 27 | |
| (oh) | 19.5 | 22.0 | 23.0 | 24.0 | | 23 | 28 | 26 | 27 | |
| (th) | 68.0 | 53.5 | 27.0 | | | 15 | 28 | 26 | | |
| (dh) | 63.5 | 44.5 | 34.0 | | | 22 | 28 | 26 | | |
| Class group 6–9 | | | | | | | | | | |
| (r) | 12.5 | 25.0 | 29.0 | 55.5 | 70.0 | 21 | 30 | 29 | 29 | 29 |
| (eh) | 27.0 | 30.0 | 34.0 | 35.0 | | 23 | 30 | 29 | 29 | |
| (oh) | 20.0 | 23.5 | 26.5 | 29.5 | | 27 | 30 | 29 | 27 | |
| (th) | 25.5 | 16.5 | 10.0 | | | 23 | 30 | 29 | | |
| (dh) | 29.5 | 16.5 | 13.0 | | | 27 | 30 | 29 | | |

*Source*: Labov 1966:221.

only style in which there is a significant difference (at $p < .05$) is style D; all the others are not significant at $p < .05$.

These results are interesting for several reasons. First, it appears that style D′ does not differentiate social classes in New York City. Second, because the major differences between the three classes exist, as one would expect, between the lowest and the highest, we have some compelling reasons for dividing the informants in different ways. For example, one could analyze the results of each of the nine classes separately. In fact, Labov does try to do so but concludes that the best division is into six classes. Figure 3–4 shows these results, with a general rise in post-vocalic /r/ constriction as the styles become more formal. The graph here does look impressive. Labov explains the jump for class 6–8 (his lower middle class) as a fairly typical phenomenon: hypercorrection. That is, because the lower middle class is the most linguistically insecure of all the classes, its members tend to use more standard forms in more formal situations.

One problem with figure 3–4, however, is that there is no way to test the various percentages. For example, the graph indicates that at style D′ the difference between class 9 and class 0 is 22 percent, but it is important to note that the numbers of informants in these groups are, respectively, eleven and seven. Class 5 contains five informants only. It has

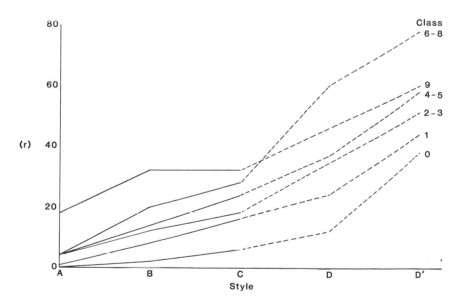

*Figure 3–4*. Redefined Class Stratification of (r): Six Class Groups (in percent). *Source*: Labov 1966:240.

been shown here that care must be exercised when drawing conclusions from such small samples. In addition, a gap of twenty percentage points between the highest and lowest classes in table 3–7 was shown not to be significant at $p < .05$. In other words, except for the obvious conclusion that figure 3–4 shows certain trends, we cannot evaluate it fully without more testing.

I do not, of course, mean to say that Labov's general conclusions about the five variables in the speech of the Lower East Side are invalid. His evidence is convincing that class stratification of these variables does exist, but it would be helpful to know just how to interpret some of the findings which are quantitatively expressed. Statistics gives us the tools, but Labov chose not to use them, and as a result some of his conclusions remain somewhat cloudy.

Moreover, in the case of figure 3–4 and many other graphs in the book as well, Labov does not present the data used to arrive at the various percentages. This omission might have serious consequences, because there is no way to calculate standard deviation. For example, we noted that class 5 contains only five people; classes 0 and 1 contain seven each; class 6 contains eight; class 9 contains eleven. In all these cases, if a few informants exhibited a large number of a certain variable, it would look as though the whole class were acting that way. Also, we saw earlier that in the example of the ages of houses in Chicago and Detroit, the difference was significant at $p < .05$ only when the samples were large. In Labov's case, we simply cannot evaluate the results adequately because they were not tested sufficiently.

In a later work (Labov 1969:731), Labov argued that one need not perform statistical tests, when results are obvious, "to determine whether or not they might have been produced by chance." If one's findings, support each other, he says, testing those findings is superfluous. The problem here, however, is knowing when the results are "obvious," and there is abundant evidence that only by performing statistical tests can we arrive at such a determination. Some scholars, especially those in the humanities, have argued with some justification that statistics in the social sciences are used for their own sake; that the statistical paraphernalia have become an end in themselves. But even if this is true for some social scientists, the fact remains that if we decide to count linguistic forms, we must test our results. Otherwise, we have no way to evaluate them. Frank Anshen has noted that "serious counting requires statistics" (1978:2). Labov's study of the English in New York City demonstrated above everything else that serious work in social dialectology does require serious counting, which inevitably leads to the rigorous testing of quantitative results so as to evaluate and interpret their meanings.

Although this section has been concerned mainly with criticizing

Labov's study, we must remember that Labov's influence on the study of social dialects has been immense, mainly because his was the first major sociolinguistic study which showed that seemingly random linguistic behavior can be patterned. The criticisms of some aspects of his method, of his not testing his findings, should not obscure the fact that his work on New York City English was monumental. Like all the studies examined thus far, it has shortcomings, but it is nonetheless a classic. It changed, as we shall see, the course of social dialectology; thereafter quantitative analysis of linguistic variation became the rule, and Labov's methods became the methods of the studies which followed.

## A Study of Social Dialects in Detroit

The first major study in which Labov's influence was apparent, *A Study of Social Dialects in Detroit* (1968), was undertaken by Roger Shuy and his associates. Like Labov's work, the Detroit study aimed at selecting a random sample, but unlike Labov's work, it found no previous sociological work on which to build. For that reason, Shuy divided metropolitan Detroit into nine areas and randomly selected one public and one private school in each. After the sample was chosen, it became clear that it did not represent the population of the city, so another sample was drawn to include, in the words of the study, "the west Detroit Polish section, the areas inhabited by recent white in-migrants from the south, some middle and upper class Negro neighborhoods, and such anomalies as the Chrysler school which is attended by poor Negro and well-to-do white children" (1968:2:3). This area was sampled using a judgment sample, called the *ethnic sample*. The first (random) sample was the *base sample*.

Thirty names were chosen at random from each base sample school and fifteen were chosen from each school in the ethnic sample. From these, ten names were chosen for interviews (we are not told how) in each base sample school and five in each ethnic sample school. The project then interviewed the child selected for the study and at least one parent or acting parent. In as many cases as possible, a teenage brother or sister was also interviewed. In all, there were 702 informants chosen, and only 7 refused to be interviewed. Perhaps because this number was so small, the Detroit study did not use a procedure equivalent to Labov's television interview; rather, the informants who refused were simply ignored.

The fieldwork was completed in ten weeks and employed eleven fieldworkers. The questionnaire was similar to that used by Labov in that there were a short-answer section, reading passages, and free conversation. It took approximately one and one-half hours to complete an interview, and each one was tape-recorded.

The social class of the informants was determined according to three criteria: education, occupation, and residence. Like Labov, Shuy used parameters established by sociologists: those of Hollingshead and Redlich, in *Social Class and Mental Illness* (1958). Each informant was ranked in the following way, for example, with regard to education:

| *Education class* | *Level of education* |
|---|---|
| 1 | Any graduate degree (professional) |
| 2 | College graduation (four years) |
| 3 | One year or more of college |
| 4 | High school graduation |
| 5 | Some high school (at least to tenth grade) |
| 6 | Junior high school (at least to seventh grade) |
| 7 | Less than seven years of school |

Similar rankings were used for profession and residence; then each ranking for each informant was multiplied by a certain factor: education by 5, profession by 9, and residence by 6. For this reason, the lower a score an informant received, the higher was the determined social class.

After all the interviews had been completed, it was decided to analyze only thirty-six of them, using the following criteria:

1. The informant had been a resident of Detroit for at least ten years.
2. The fieldworker felt that the informant was representative.
3. The fieldworker felt that the interview had been successful.
4. There was enough taped material from the interview to be analyzed.

This sample for the Detroit study, then, is clearly a judgment sample, but the above criteria probably did not bias the sample. These thirty-six informants were ranked into four social classes: group I (with scores based on the ranking system from 20 to 49), group II (with scores from

50 to 79), group III (with scores from 80 to 109), and group IV (with scores from 110 to 134).

It was decided to analyze two grammatical variables and one phonological one. The former were multiple negation (*I don't make no money no more*) and pronominal apposition (*That guy, he likes you*). The phonological variable was the realization of /m/, /n/, and/or /ŋ/ as a nasalized vowel ([θɪŋ] becoming [θĩ]). Like Labov's study before it, the study of Detroit speech revealed that people are inconsistent in their linguistic behavior but that such inconsistency follows certain patterns. Standard English forms increased as style levels became more formal and as social class became higher. The study also tried to correlate linguistic behavior with other factors such as the age and sex of the informants and found, it was argued, that children are generally more nonstandard in their speech than adults and that males are more nonstandard than females.

The following figures show that Shuy followed Labov's technique in graphing results, and we shall examine them in some detail. Table 3–8 shows the findings, by informant, for multiple negation. The number of informants in each of the four groups is also indicated. Figure 3–5 shows the social stratification of the variable.

The various percentages in figure 3–5 were derived in a rather interesting way. One might assume that the Detroit investigators used the data in table 3–8 to set up a frequency distribution and that the means in figure 3–5 represent the average percentage for each group. In fact, such is not the case; instead, the total number of potential double negatives was counted, then the total actual number. The percentages in figure 3–5 are the result of dividing the total actual responses for each group by the total potential responses for that group.

This procedure assumes that the data for the four groups are homogeneous, but an examination of table 3–8 reveals that they are not. In group II, we see that fully six of eleven informants used no double negatives at all, and of five informants in group I, only one used a double negative and then used it only once. If we calculate the frequencies for the groups, not assuming homogeneity, we can also calculate standard deviations and perform the *t*-test. If we do so for figure 3–5, we find that first of all, the mean percentage of group II is 18.22 (not 11.1), and the mean for group III is 41.17 (not 38.1). The two standard deviations are, respectively, 32.77 and 34.44 percent, and the *t*-test reveals that the difference between groups II and III is not significant at $p < .05$; $t = 1.689$, so the level of significance is as high as $p < .20$, a 20 percent uncertainty, which is clearly unacceptable.

The procedure used to arrive at the percentages permits any one informant to influence the results for his entire group unduly. For example, of a total of fifty-one actual double negatives in group III, tapes

*Table 3–8.* Double Negatives by Informant's Social Rank

| Social rank | Informant | | | | Double negative | | |
|---|---|---|---|---|---|---|---|
| | Tape no. | Sex | Age | Race | Potential | Realized | % |
| | | | | Group I | | | |
| 20 | 95 | F | 13 | W | 5 | 0 | — |
| 32 | 388 | M | 42 | N | 16 | 1 | 6.3 |
| 37 | 41 | F | 43 | W | 23 | 0 | — |
| 41 | 88 | F | 41 | W | 10 | 0 | — |
| 43 | 347 | F | 10 | W | 5 | 0 | — |
| 54 | 499 | F | 11 | W | 8 | 1 | 12.5 |
| | | | | Group II | | | |
| 54 | 284 | F | 10 | W | 15 | 0 | — |
| 59 | 575 | F | 42 | W | 5 | 0 | — |
| 60 | 101 | F | 15 | W | 14 | 0 | — |
| 71 | 300 | M | 38 | W | 12 | 7 | 62.5 |
| 74 | 243 | M | 9 | W | 9 | 1 | 11.1 |
| 74 | 281 | F | 20 | W | 2 | 0 | — |
| 74 | 283 | F | 10 | W | 17 | 0 | — |
| 77 | 128 | M | 15 | N | 14 | 2 | 14.3 |
| 78 | 92 | F | 11 | W | 7 | 0 | — |
| 78 | 649 | M | 10 | N | 2 | 2 | 100.0 |

## Group III

| | | | | | | | |
|---|---|---|---|---|---|---|---|
| 80 | 141 | F | 16 | N | 11 | 0 | — |
| 92 | 596 | M | 15 | W | 15 | 8 | 53.3 |
| 97 | 137 | F | 10 | W | 8 | 1 | 12.5 |
| 97 | 208 | F | 31 | W | 12 | 3 | 25.0 |
| 97 | 305 | M | 35 | N | 32 | 11 | 34.4 |
| 98 | 401 | M | 10 | N | 4 | 0 | — |
| 99 | 648 | F | 11 | W | 6 | 4 | 66.7 |
| 102 | 256 | F | 12 | N | 2 | 1 | 50.0 |
| 103 | 445 | M | 38 | W | 9 | 1 | 11.1 |
| 103 | 15 | M | 10 | N | 4 | 4 | 100.0 |
| 104 | 193 | F | 12 | N | 5 | 4 | 80.0 |
| 108 | 65 | F | 12 | W | 6 | 0 | — |
| 108 | 230 | F | 13 | N | 9 | 8 | 88.9 |
| 109 | 315 | M | 12 | N | 11 | 6 | 54.5 |

## Group IV

| | | | | | | | |
|---|---|---|---|---|---|---|---|
| 111 | 565 | F | 14 | N | 17 | 16 | 94.1 |
| 113 | 214 | F | 32 | N | 18 | 5 | 27.8 |
| 120 | 491 | F | 10 | W | 6 | 2 | 33.3 |
| 122 | 403 | F | 11 | W | 10 | 7 | 70.0 |
| 129 | 237 | F | 9 | N | 5 | 3 | 60.0 |
| 134 | 506 | M | 48 | N | 32 | 29 | 90.6 |

*Source:* Shuy 1968:III:10.

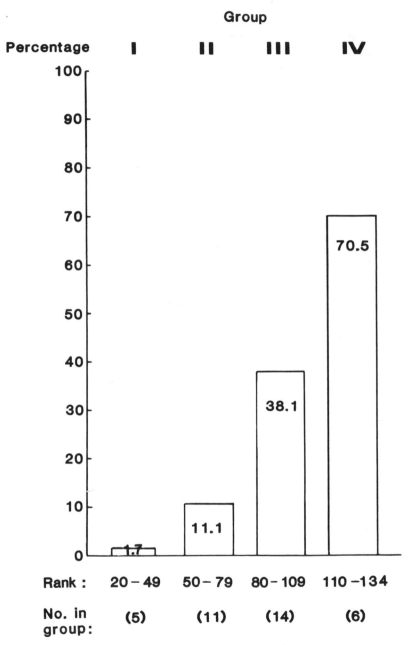

*Figure 3–5*. Multiple Negation: Social Classification, All Informants (Mean Percentages). *Source*: Shuy 1968:III:12.

305, 108, and 109 (about 20 percent of the group) account for almost half. On the other hand, of a total of 134 potential double negatives for group III, tapes 141, 208, 305, and 596 (28.5 percent of the group) are responsible for 52 percent. A frequency distribution and standard deviation would have revealed this disproportion to a great extent.

Figure 3–6 provides the basis for the following comment: "It appears that there is a distinct contrast between all four groups" (1968:3:15). Again, however, even the contrast between the middle two groups is not significant at $p < .05$. An examination of table 3–8 reveals that of twenty-nine actual double negatives from group III informants aged thirteen and older, eleven of them came from only one informant (tape 305). His tape, plus that of tape 596, account for more than one-half of the total actual responses for the group as a whole. In other words, the $t$-test shows that the difference in figure 3–6 between the middle two groups is not significant because the standard deviations are so high. Once more we see that graphs and tables do not speak for themselves; they must be evaluated and interpreted.

Another interesting aspect of the Detroit project is what was called the "structural frequency study," an attempt to determine if there is a correlation between social class and/or age with the kinds and numbers of clause patterns used. The study chose four informants for this part of the analysis:

1. a white female adult with a social class rank of 37 (group I)
2. a black female adult with a social class rank of 97 (group III)
3. a white female child with a social class rank of 97 (group III)
4. a black male child with a social class rank of 103 (group IV)

[3A:2]

The clause patterns in the speech of these four were then analyzed to determine possible relationships, and it was argued that the informant with the highest social class rank (group I) had the most linguistic structures.

Table 3–9 shows the results for relative embedding, in sentences such as "the man *who was here* . . . ," "the man *I saw* . . . ," or "the man *with a hat* came" (a transformation of "the man *who has a hat* came"). Chi-square tests on these data reveal that informant 41 does indeed use more relative embedding than the others do, at a level of significance of $p < .01$. Here statistical tests support Shuy's conclusions. The Detroit study also concluded that age and race were not determining factors in structural frequency but cautioned that the sample of four informants was too small to make any of the conclusions ironclad.

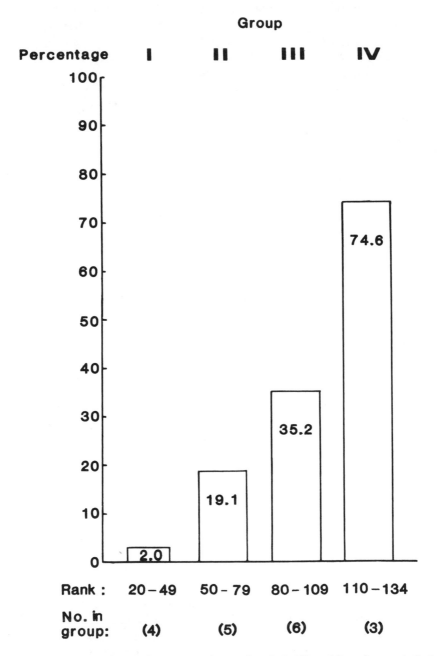

*Figure 3–6.* Multiple Negation: Social Classification, Adult
Informants (Mean Percentages). *Source*: Shuy 1968:III:15.

*Table 3–9.* Results for Relative Embedding

| Group | Informant 15 Occ./total | % | Informant 41 Occ./total | % | Informant 137 Occ./total | % | Informant 208 Occ./total | % |
|---|---|---|---|---|---|---|---|---|
| I | 25/230 | 10.9 | 39/184 | 27.2 | 20/155 | 12.9 | 9/139 | 6.5 |
| II | — | — | 6/12 | 50.0 | —/11 | .0 | 2/16 | 12.5 |
| III | — | — | 1/4 | 25.0 | — | — | — | — |
| IV | 25/357 | 7.0 | 82/681 | 12.0 | 18/326 | 5.5 | 18/330 | 5.5 |
| V | 1/5 | 20.0 | 3/13 | 23.1 | 2/110 | 1.8 | —/9 | .0 |
| VI | 2/16 | 12.5 | 10/27 | 37.0 | 3/20 | 15.0 | 1/18 | 5.5 |
| VII | — | — | — | — | — | — | — | — |
| VIII | 39/74 | 52.7 | 17/28 | 60.7 | 16/27 | 59.3 | 5/35 | 14.3 |
| IX | 10/48 | 20.4 | 38/113 | 33.6 | 18/58 | 31.0 | 25/75 | 33.3 |
| X | 5/79 | 6.3 | 42/234 | 17.9 | 8/96 | 8.3 | 12/88 | 13.6 |
| XI | 6/37 | 16.2 | 23/110 | 20.9 | 12/50 | 24.0 | 11/67 | 15.9 |
| XII | — | — | — | — | —/1 | .0 | — | — |
| XIII | — | — | — | — | 1/1 | 100.0 | — | — |
| XIV | —/17 | .0 | 5/36 | 13.9 | —/15 | .0 | —/5 | .0 |
| XV | —/9 | .0 | 13/47 | 27.7 | 4/22 | 18.2 | 3/17 | 17.7 |
| XVI | 1/9 | 1.1 | 3/14 | 21.4 | 4/27 | 47.7 | 1/12 | 8.3 |
| Total | 114/878 | 12.8 | 282/1500 | 18.8 | 106/820 | 12.9 | 87/813 | 10.7 |

*Note:* Occ. = actual occurrences. Total = total possible occurrences.
*Source:* Shuy 1968:III:11.

The Detroit study, more so than the study of New York City, was aimed particularly at teachers. Its aim was to identify speech forms which are socially relevant. The study also argues that standard English should be taught as a second dialect in much the same way that second languages are taught and that such programs focus on socially significant aspects of the speech of lower-class students. If a person can change those features in his speech which "mark" him as lower class, his language will not be a barrier to his social and professional mobility: "Identification of the appropriate variants may be the best identifiers of the substance of good teaching. The ultimate choice of when to use certain variants and when not to use them will have to be made by the speaker. Teachers can't legislate virtue, no matter how they define it. But they can, and must, provide the linguistic alternatives" (1968:3B:23–24).

The Detroit study was never actually published. It remains in the form of a report to the U.S. Office of Education, Department of Health, Education and Welfare. We shall now turn to a published study based on the findings of the Detroit project. *A Sociolinguistic Description of Detroit Negro Speech* (1969).

## A Sociolinguistic Description of Detroit Negro Speech

Walter A. Wolfram, one of Shuy's colleagues for the Detroit project, chose forty-eight black informants from those interviewed by the Detroit fieldworkers. These informants were evenly divided into the four social classes used by the previous study, and each group of twelve was further divided into three age groups: four informants aged ten to twelve, four aged fourteen to seventeen, and four aged thirty to fifty-five. In addition to these forty-eight, Wolfram selected twelve white informants of the highest social class in the Detroit project; they, too, were evenly divided by age and sex. In other words, Wolfram analyzed the speech of sixty informants, twenty-four of whom (twelve white and twelve black) were upper middle class and thirty-six of whom were black and were evenly divided into three social classes: lower middle, upper working, and lower working.

Wolfram's linguistic variables were both phonological and grammatical. On the phonological side, he analyzed (1) simplification of final consonant clusters in such words as *test, wasp,* and *left,* (2) the pronunciation of medial and final /θ/ in such words as *tooth* and *nothing,* (3) syllable final /d/ in words like *good* and *shed,* and (4) postvocalic /r/ in words like *sister* and *fair.* His grammatical variables were (1) the zero copula (*she nice*), (2) invariant *be* (*I be twelve February seven*), (3) suffixal {-Z} [(*he talk(s), John('s) book, three year(s)*], and (4) multiple negation. Wolfram's goal was to correlate the use of these variables with social class, age, and sex, and in line with previous research, he found that nonstandard speech increases as social class decreases, that generally males are more nonstandard in their speech than females, and that younger speakers are more nonstandard than older ones. Of course, many of the conclusions are not so clear-cut and simply stated, but this general pattern does emerge from the study.

For example, when Wolfram counted the number of times the sound /θ/ was replaced by /f/, /t/, or Ø (zero), he obtained the results in figure 3–7. UMN is "upper middle [class] negro," UWN is "upper working [class] negro," and so on. He argued: "The combined percentage of *f, t,* or Ø realization for 24 female informants is approximately 10 per cent lower than the 24 males (34.9 per cent . . . for the females as opposed to 44.7 for the males). The females come closer to approximating the SE [standard English] norm than the males do" (1969:91–92).

Similarly, as figure 3–8 indicates, the percentage of the simplification of final consonant clusters in monosyllables seems to increase as social class becomes lower.

Like Labov and Shuy, Wolfram did not test the reliability of his findings, and in some cases, graphs such as that shown in figure 3–7 can

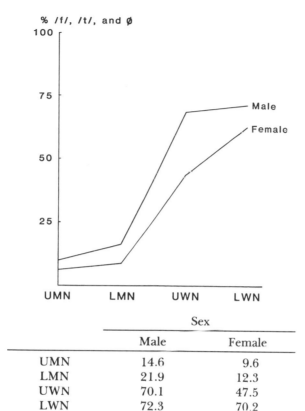

| Sex | | |
| --- | --- | --- |
| | Male | Female |
| UMN | 14.6 | 9.6 |
| LMN | 21.9 | 12.3 |
| UWN | 70.1 | 47.5 |
| LWN | 72.3 | 70.2 |

*Figure 3–7.* Percentage of /f/, /t/, and Ø Realization, /θ/ Variable. *Source*: Wolfram 1969:92.

be somewhat misleading. First of all, Wolfram took fifteen potential pronunciations of /θ/ for each informant; since there are six informants in each group, he was working with a total of ninety potential /θ/ for each of the classes. For the upper-middle-class black group, then, he obtained a total of approximately thirteen responses for the men that were not /θ/ and approximately nine for the women. These numbers are approximate, because neither 14.6 percent of ninety nor 9.6 percent of ninety is a whole number. Wolfram probably used either fewer or more than ninety potential /θ/ for the whole groups, but we have no way of knowing. He says (1969:83) that he used fifteen potential /θ/ for each informant, however. In any case, there exists the possibility that, for both the males and the females, one informant could have been responsible for all of the actual /θ/ of his or her class. Since no frequency distribution is

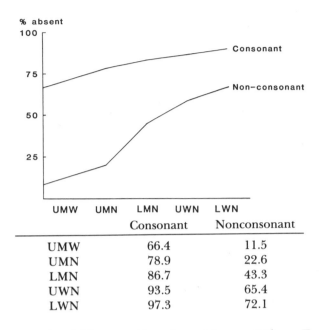

| | Consonant | Nonconsonant |
|---|---|---|
| UMW | 66.4 | 11.5 |
| UMN | 78.9 | 22.6 |
| LMN | 86.7 | 43.3 |
| UWN | 93.5 | 65.4 |
| LWN | 97.3 | 72.1 |

*Figure 3–8.* Final Cluster Member Absent When Followed by Consonantal and Nonconsonantal Environments (in percent). *Source:* Wolfram 1969:68.

presented, there is no way to determine just how homogeneous the sample results were.

Although we cannot evaluate completely the results in figure 3–7, we can use the percentages for each sex and perform a *t*-test for the significance of the 10 percent difference between the males and the females. Here, as Wolfram points out, the means are 44.7 for the men and 34.9 for the women. The standard deviations are, respectively, 30.73 and 29.19 percent. The *t*-test reveals that the results are significant at $p < .40$, far below the minimum $p < .05$. On the other hand, the mean percentages for the blacks of the upper working class do look impressive: 70.1 percent for the men and 47.5 percent for the women. It is conceivable that a *t*-test on those data would reveal a significant ($p < .05$) difference here, but the information necessary for the calculation of the test is not provided; that is, one would need the individual scores of each of the twelve informants involved. Similarly, the findings in figure 3–8 are also impressive, but a test of the results would have permitted us to determine the level of significance at which they are valid. The number of informants in each class (twelve) is too small to permit the use of the proportion test.

In spite of these difficulties with Wolfram's methods of analysis, his book yields an overall impression similar to those of Labov and Shuy. There is a relationship between language variety and social class, age, and sex. Since almost all of Wolfram's findings indicate such a relationship, the paucity of statistical testing only means that we do not know how significant, in terms of probabilities, the results are. Wolfram's conclusions about these various relationships seem valid, however; the only problem is knowing in precise terms just how valid they are. Graphs such as that in figure 3–9 are convincing indeed. In other words, the main difficulty with *A Sociolinguistic Description of Detroit Negro Speech* is a mat-

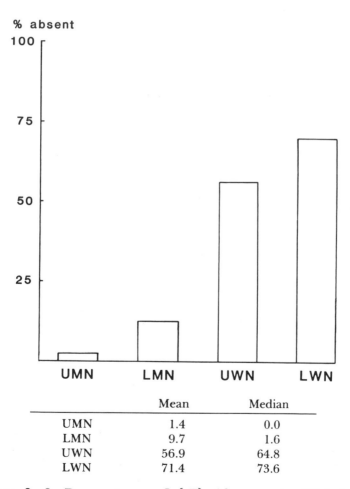

| | Mean | Median |
|---|---|---|
| UMN | 1.4 | 0.0 |
| LMN | 9.7 | 1.6 |
| UWN | 56.9 | 64.8 |
| LWN | 71.4 | 73.6 |

*Figure 3–9.* Percentage of {-Z} Absence in Third-Person Singular Present Tense Concord. *Source*: Wolfram 1969:36.

ter of method: a certain lack of scientific rigor. The book is impressive
for what it does show in spite of these shortcomings.

Wolfram's work can be understood fully, however, only if it is seen in a
larger context; the controversy over the nature of Black English, which
started in the mid-1960s and which has only recently been substantially
resolved. As we shall see, Wolfram's research, based as it was on the
Detroit dialect project, was the first large-scale published research which
dealt with the provenance and identity of the dialects spoken by black
Americans.

## The Question of Black English

One of the first dialects of English spoken by black Americans to
receive scholarly attention was *Gullah*. Gullah is spoken mainly on the
islands off the Georgia and South Carolina coast and is unique in many
ways for the African influence it shows. Gullah speakers are the descendants of slaves who were brought to North America in the eighteenth and
nineteenth centuries. Because they were so isolated, their language developed perhaps differently from any other variety of English now
spoken in the United States, and it is generally regarded as a *creole*
language.

Put simply, a creole is a very special kind of language, the result of
contact between peoples who speak different languages in, usually, a
condition of imperialism. To be specific, we know that the slaves brought
to North America from West Africa did speak a number of different
languages: Twi, Hausa, Mandingo, Meninka, Fanti, and many others.
These are not dialects of a single language but rather separate languages. The people who spoke them were thrown together by the institution of slavery, and often, in fact, it was the policy of the slave
traders to try to make sure that people from the same tribes were not
sold to the same owner. This practice meant, of course, that when slaves
reached their destinations on the rice, indigo, and cotton plantations
along the South Carolina and Georgia coasts, they were frequently un-
able to communicate with the vast majority of their fellow sufferers. The
language spoken by their masters was English, and at the beginning the
slaves who were the ancestors of today's Gullahs learned a simplified
variety of English which they could use to communicate with both their
overseers and the slaves who spoke other languages. This simplified
language is usually called a *pidgin*, and it is spoken for specific purposes
of communication by people who also know a "regular" language. For
example, a speaker of Hausa would use his native language with other

Hausa speakers but would use the pidgin with most of the people with whom he came in contact.

As time passed, however, the following generation of slaves began to lose their native languages, and in the Gullah country, at least, they began to speak the pidgin as a native language. When that happens, linguists call the results a *creole*, a former pidgin learned as a native language. Like pidgins, the creole languages have a simplified grammar, vocalic systems, and other features. For example, most English-based creoles make no distinction between subject and object pronouns, and there are very few grammatical inflections.

The first study of Gullah was John Bennett's (1908), but as the following quotation indicates, Bennett had no knowledge of the process of creolization; instead, he attributed the Gullah dialect to his own conception of the people themselves: "Intellectual indolence, or laziness, mental and physical, which shows itself in the shortening of words, the elision of syllables, and modification of every difficult pronunciation" (1908:40). This comment, though far from scientific, was typical of remarks about Gullah until later in this century, when Lorenzo Turner published what has by now become a classic work: *Africanisms in the Gullah Dialect* (1948).

First of all, Turner demonstrated that the vocabulary of the Gullah dialect is filled with words whose origin can be traced to several African languages. Moreover, although Turner himself did not stress the fact, his work revealed linguistic structures in Gullah which also exist in other creoles of the Western Hemisphere. The so-called simplified vowel system may, in fact, be the result of the influence of several West African languages. But the most important contribution of Turner's work is that, as far as Gullah is concerned, at least, it refuted claims such as the following, by George Phillip Krapp, one of the first modern historians of American English: "The Negroes, indeed, in acquiring English have done their work so thoroughly that they have retained not a trace of any native African speech" (1924:190).

For the most part, dialectologists have tended to treat Gullah as somehow different from the dialects spoken by other black Americans. They regard Gullah as a unique phenomenon. In his *Word Geography of the Eastern United States*, Kurath wrote: "By and large the Southern Negro speaks the language of the white man of his locality or area and of his education. . . . As far as the speech of uneducated Negroes is concerned, it differs little from that of the illiterate white; that is, it exhibits the same regional and local variations as that of the simple white folk" (1949:6).

The first American dialectologists to suggest that there may be African language influence in the dialects of black Americans were Virginia and

Raven McDavid, in their article "The Relationship of the Speech of American Negroes to the Speech of Whites" (1951). The McDavids observed that the discipline of anthropology, which heavily influenced the course of American linguistics, should prevent us from making ethnocentric and racist statements such as that by Bennett above. Moreover, the McDavids noted that work on African languages, then recently initiated, gives perspective to the study of the English spoken by blacks. They suggested that some features in the phonology, morphology, and syntax of American black speech may be *"the persistence of something from African speech"* (1951; quoted from Wolfram and Clarke 1971:22; italics in the original).

Creolization was also suggested by the McDavids (1951) as a possible direction for the study of Black English:

> ... the research into Taki-Taki, Brazilian Negro Portuguese, and Haitian Creole enables the student of American Negro speech to assay whether a particular structural feature is of African origin or not. If a certain feature of Gullah syntax, say, is also found in Brazilian Negro Portuguese, in Haitian Creole, and in Papiamento, and resembles a structural feature of several West African languages, it is likely that it is not taken from British peasant speech. [1971:22–23]

They also argued that black speech should be studied without preconceptions, to determine "whether a form found among Negroes in the South is likely to be African or folk English in origin" (1971:29).

At the time of the McDavids' article, the evidence from linguistic atlas field records supported, with few reservations, the statement by Kurath quoted above: for all practical purposes, blacks and whites of the same socioeconomic class in the South speak essentially the same. The McDavids suggested that the uniqueness of Gullah can be explained because of the isolation of Gullah speakers from the white community. Moreover, they noted a number of words from African languages which have found their way into the national idiom: *gumbo, voodoo, jigger* (*chigger*), *bad mouth*. The list of regional expressions in the South is longer still, but the general conclusion reached by the McDavids is that, although there may be relics in the speech of blacks, there are no significant differences between their speech and that of whites. Their article did, however, suggest the direction of future research, especially in the area of the relationship between black speech and creole languages and African languages.

The 1950s and the 1960s saw continued research on African languages and, more importantly for our purposes, on creole languages. In 1965, Beryl Loftman Bailey, herself a native speaker of Jamaican Creole, published "Toward a New Perspective in Negro English Dialectology" and argued that the English of uneducated black people is, in fact, a different *language* from that of whites. The English of lower-class blacks, she suggested, has its roots in an early creole language: "I would like to suggest that the Southern Negro 'dialect' differs from other Southern speech because its deep structure is different, having its origins as it undoubtedly does in some Proto-Creole grammatical structure" (Wolfram and Clarke 1971:43).

Because, as Bailey admitted, she is not a native speaker of American English, she used the literary dialect found in the speech of Duke, a character in Warren Miller's novel *The Cool World* (1959). Bailey argued that there are structural similarities between Duke's speech and Jamaican Creole and that these similarities suggest a creole ancestor for the speech of uneducated black Southerners. Bailey pointed out, of course, that evidence from literary dialect is hardly conclusive, but she did urge that the creole theory be pursued and that linguists investigate the idea.

One of the first linguists to do so was William Stewart, who in 1967 published "Sociolinguistic Factors in the History of American Negro Dialects." According to Stewart, there is evidence in written sources from the American colonial period which suggests that Bailey's position is valid. Stewart's evidence indicates that a pidginized form of English was quite widespread among the slaves in the eighteenth century, especially among those who worked in the fields rather than in the house. The slaves who were attached in one way or another to domestic work learned a variety of English which was more standard, mainly because of their proximity to the white plantation owners, and according to Stewart there was a "social cleavage" between them and the field hands. After the Civil War, the abolition of slavery meant that even the field hands received more education. As a result their language "began to lose many of its creole characteristics, and take on more and more of the features of the local white dialects and of the written language" (1967; quoted from Wolfram and Clarke 1971:84). There remain today, according to Stewart, only a few vestiges of that early creole. One of Stewart's best known examples is "invariant *be*" as opposed to copula absence; Stewart argued that there is a distinction in the speech of lower-class black people between *he busy* ("he's busy at this moment") and *he be busy* ("he's busy all the time").

In a later article (1968), Stewart suggested that there are structural similarities between nonstandard black speech and Gullah. He gives the following example (quoted from Wolfram and Clarke 1971), where STE is standard English, WNS is white nonstandard, NNS is black nonstandard, and GUL is Gullah:

```
STE:  We were eating—and drinking, too.
WNS:  We was eatin'—and drinkin', too.
NNS:  We was eatin'—and we drinkin', too.
GUL:  We bin duh nyam—en' we duh drink, too.
```

[P. 60]

Stewart suggests that the similarities here between WNS and NNS are only a matter of "word-form similarities" (1971:60) and that in fact the repetition of the *we* in both NNS and GUL is evidence for similar structures. Moreover, Stewart cites data from three other contact languages to support his point. In the example below, JMC is Jamaican Creole, SRA is the creole spoken in Surinam, in South America, and WAP is West African Pidgin English:

```
JMC:  We ben a nyam—an' we a drink, too.
SRA:  We ben de nyang—en we de dringie, too.
WAP:  We bin de eat—an' we de dring, too.
```

[1971:62]

Stewart rightly argues that "these correspondences are much too neat to be dismissed as mere accident" (1971:62).

The essential question here is Stewart's assertion that NNS does in fact repeat the personal pronoun. No evidence from fieldwork is presented. In other words, even if the early creole did exist, and Stewart's evidence is such that it probably did, we must still ask whether the nonstandard dialects spoken by black people today continue to show vestiges of that creole to the extent that such dialects have a different underlying structure from the dialects spoken by whites. In any case, we can see a wide divergence in scholarly opinion concerning the dialects of black Americans. The McDavids, while noting African *influence* on southern speech in general and black speech in particular, suggested that blacks and whites in the South speak essentially the same, depending on socioeconomic class. Stewart and Bailey, on the other hand, argued for the separate linguistic identity of Black English.

We noted the nature of the evidence used by the two sides in this controversy. The McDavids used atlas field records; Bailey used literary dialect and her knowledge of Jamaican Creole; Stewart used his knowledge of several creole languages, including Gullah but had no evidence from a corpus insofar as Black English is concerned. In addition, the kinds of differences between black speech and white which were pointed out by Bailey and Stewart were not to be found in linguistic atlas field records, and it seemed clear enough that the issue could not be resolved without additional research.

As the decade of the 1960s progressed into the 1970s, the question of the identity of the dialects spoken by black Americans remained open. Dialectologists in the atlas tradition continued to argue that the only differences between the dialects of the two races were quantitative in nature; that, in the South at least, certain forms were more frequent in the speech of blacks than in that of whites but that there were no important qualitative differences (see McDavid and Davis 1972). The creolists, on the other hand, maintained their position and sometimes did so virulently (see especially Dillard 1972, 1975, in this regard), but very little research was carried out by either group on the question at hand. It took the dialectologists in the Labov tradition, who carried out large-scale quantitative studies on the language of blacks, to help resolve the issue.

The Detroit dialect project included black informants of all social classes, and Labov and his associates (1968) studied the English of black and Puerto Rican speakers in New York City. Both of these projects, however, remained unpublished, so the first major study of Black English is Wolfram's (1969) work, based on the Detroit field records. Wolfram found that there are certain rules for copula deletion, for example, which are applicable only to black speech but that these rules are surface in nature. In this he was following Labov, who in 1968 read a paper at the Conference on Pidginization and Creolization of Languages in Jamaica and claimed that the deletion of the verb *be* could be predicted by rule (the paper was later published as Labov 1969). The very use of the word *deletion* suggests that the verb *be* must be considered a part of the underlying structure of the English of lower-class black people, and thus, in effect, Labov did not support Stewart and Bailey concerning the creole substratum theory. Wolfram's data supported those of Labov, but it should be stressed that Wolfram's data on black-white speech differences were not particularly amenable to comparison. That is, Wolfram did not include working-class whites, recent in-migrants to Detroit from the South, for comparison with working-class blacks. Clearly some research in the South was needed to determine whether differences between black speech and white speech are qualitative or quantitative in nature—and, of course, just what those differences are.

A beginning was made by Wolfram, Shuy, and Ralph Fasold, in Holmes County, Mississippi (Wolfram 1971). They interviewed fifty children, twenty-five white and twenty-five black, ranging from six to eight years of age. And they found differences. For example, even though both races said things like *he do*, black children did so far more often than did the whites; in fact, a number of black informants used no inflection at all, whereas among the whites, the zero inflection always varied with the standard form. Other differences were found as well,

mainly quantitative in nature or involving different linguistic environments where forms occur in black speech and not in white.

The work by Shuy, Wolfram, and Fasold tended to support the position of the atlas dialectologists more than that of the creolists. First of all,
the Holmes County data did not bear out Stewart's claim concerning the
distinction between *he tired* and *he be tired*: "In our data, we observe *He
busy all the time* as well as *He busy right now* (or its alternative *He is busy right
now*). The conclusion, then, is that there is a Black-White speech differentiation with reference to the copula in the South, but it is on a
relatively superficial level of language structure" (Wolfram 1971:150–
51). Although the Holmes County data did not support the creole substratum theory that Black English has a different underlying structure
from white English, the findings did reveal genuine differences between
the linguistic behavior of the two races. It is possible that these are the
result of African language influence or, for that matter, early creole
influence, but to claim influence is far weaker than to claim an underlying structure of Black English which is different from that of whites.

Wolfram himself notes the problems involved in using exclusively
informants who are six to eight years old. Clearly, some of the features
in their speech might simply be a function of the continuing language-
learning process. On the other hand, the Holmes County project was the
first comparative research on black and white speech in the South, and it
is valuable for that reason. It was also preliminary, in many ways, to a
more ambitious study published by Wolfram in 1974. After conducting
more than 100 interviews in Franklin County, Mississippi, Wolfram decided to concentrate on some forty-four white informants from the
working class. These were divided into the following age groups:
(1) eight to ten years, (2) eleven to thirteen years, and (3) sixteen to
seventeen years. In addition, Wolfram added a small number of middle-
class informants to determine, in his words, the "local informal standard" (1974a:501).

The Franklin County findings provided no major surprises. As was
the case in Holmes County, Wolfram found that whites do omit the
copula and use uninflected *be* but that they generally do so in linguistic
environments which are different from those found for black speech.
Moreover, Wolfram suggests that one can separate the question of
whether a creole once existed among slaves from that of whether black
speech is different, in some respects, from white speech. He does conclude that there is reason to believe that particularly invariant *be*, as it is
used in lower-class black speech, may be a leftover from an early creole,
and he goes on to suggest that the absence of the verb *be* in white speech
may be a result of black influence.

If Wolfram was right, then, the argument between the creolists and dialectologists in the atlas tradition was on its way to resolution. The dialectologists were correct in their assertion that black-white speech differences are essentially quantitative in nature, and some of the creolists were correct as well, since they argued that blacks used certain forms differently from whites. There were certain problems, however, with the Franklin County study which meant that the issue could not be completely resolved there. For one thing, none of Wolfram's results were subjected to rigorous testing, so the reader cannot know at what level of significance the findings are valid. Moreover, Wolfram's decision not to include older speakers from the working class is unfortunate, since however interesting the language of children and teenagers may be, it cannot be taken as necessarily representative of the language of their social class as a whole.

This problem was remedied, to a large extent, by the work of Crawford Feagin (1979) in Anniston, Alabama, a city with a population of about 60,000. All of Feagin's approximately eighty informants were white and were divided into two major social classes: upper and working. In addition, she divided her working-class informants into two subgroups: urban and rural. These classes were, in turn, divided and classified by both sex and age (teenagers and people over sixty). One of the main goals of her study was to determine if there exist forms in black speech which do not exist in white speech; her data for black speech came from Labov and associates (1968), Labov (1972), Wolfram (1969, 1974a), Fasold (1972), and other sources as well. Feagin's work is the first large-scale published study of the speech of a southern community.

Perhaps because most of the claims for the uniqueness of uneducated black speech deal with morphology and syntax, all of Feagin's (1979) linguistic variables are in these areas. She examined features such as invariant *be*, absence of the copula, tense, voice, and aspect, and her conclusion is worth quoting here at some length:

> Altogether, so far as the verb phrase is concerned, Southern White English, especially Nonstandard Southern White, and Black English remain quantitatively somewhat different, but quite similar in their syntax, the main difference lying in the subject-verb agreement for finite verbs. This is not to say that they are exactly the same. The semantics of Black English verbs seems to be qualitatively different, despite striking parallels. Still, it does not seem farfetched to claim that two people of disparate origins, after 250 to 300 years of living together, now share a common language encompassing near-standard at one end, with individuals of either race scattered all the way from most standard to least standard, but with the whites as a group concentrated between the completely standard

end and the second quartile and the blacks as a group concentrated at the nonstandard end up to the third quartile. The important point is that it is a single system. [P. 257]

Feagin also points out, however, that certain forms and usages which occur only marginally at best among the Anniston informants do occur with high frequency in the speech of blacks, and she suggests that since these forms have analogues in certain creole languages, they can be viewed as "undoubtedly remnants of Creole" (1979:263).

Feagin's study, then, comes close to resolving the controversy over the identity of Black English; however, just as many of the studies of the language of urban blacks in the North did not include whites of southern origins for comparison, so Feagin did not sample the language of the black residents of Anniston. Instead, she used data from the northern urban studies, and it is at least possible that the speech of northern blacks in well-established communities has developed differently from that of blacks still living in the South. In other words, the comparative data from the South are still needed before the issue can be resolved once and for all, but Feagin's research has gone a long way toward providing that solution.

There is yet another aspect of Feagin's book which must be noted here: she tests her findings using chi-square. For example, table 3–10 shows her results for a comparison of the informants in her two classes who use *done* before past participles, as in *you've done spent your five dollars*. Her reasons for using statistical tests are convincing, especially in light of what we have seen earlier in this chapter:

> . . . it is necessary to define environments in which the variables occur, to count items, to figure percentages, to use statistics. Certain items, of course, are more amenable to counting than others, since generally the technique is to count the cases of occurrence and nonoccurrence of a certain structure. . . . It is only through such close attention to the data, rejecting impressionistic or intuitive interpretations, that it is possible to

*Table 3–10.* Chi-Square Test for Double Modals

| Informant group | Yes | Exp | No | Exp | Total |
|---|---|---|---|---|---|
| Upper class | 2 | 5.27 | 30 | 26.73 | 32 |
| Working class | 11 | 7.73 | 36 | 39.27 | 47 |
| Total | 13 | — | 66 | — | 79 |

*Note:* $\chi^2 = 4.08$, $df = 1$, $p < .05$.          Exp = expected.
*Source:* Feagin 1979:155.

arrive at a real conception of how language works. Otherwise we are left with hazy ideas of self-fulfilling intuitions, which distort any serious or careful (or scientific) discussion of language. [P. 22]

We noted above the comment by Anshen (1978:2) that "serious counting requires statistics." Feagin's point is essentially the same; statistics are required by serious social dialectology whenever the counting of the occurrence and nonoccurrence of variables is involved. Whenever she can, Feagin uses the chi-square test, and as table 3–11 shows, sometimes mere impressions of differences are not particularly revealing. In other places, the differences between, in this case, the linguistic behavior of the two sexes is significant, and statistics provides the answers.

Unfortunately, there are certain problems with Feagin's use of the chi-square test, not the least of which is the fact that some of the results in table 3–11 are presented incorrectly. For example, in the case of multiple negation, she notes that a chi-square test of the findings for the males and females of her older rural working-class informants yields a value of 9.00, with a level of significance of $p < .01$. For the older urban informants, her chi-square value is higher still (9.92), yet here she says that the level of significance is only $p < .05$; we know that, at each degree of freedom, the higher the value of chi-square, the more valid the results are. In addition, a look at table 3–5 reveals that, at one degree of freedom, any chi-square value above 6.635 gives a level of confidence of $p < .01$, far better than Feagin indicates for either test of her findings

*Table 3–11.* Chi-Square Scores for Sex Differences

| Feature | Older rural | | Older urban | | Teen urban | |
|---|---|---|---|---|---|---|
| | $x^2$ | $p$ | $x^2$ | $p$ | $x^2$ | $p$ |
| Invariable *don't* | 0 | (n.s.) | 4.82 | (n.s.) | .97 | (n.s.) |
| Multiple negation | 9.00 | .01[a] | 9.92 | .05[b] | 2.28 | (n.s.) |
| Invariable *was* | .82 | (n.s.) | .38 | (n.s.) | 25.47 | .01[a] |
| NP plural + $-s$ | 17.38 | .01[b] | 4.35 | (n.s.) | 5.38 | .05[a] |
| Invariable *is* | 3.58 | (n.s.) | .45 | (n.s.) | 1.19 | (n.s.) |
| *Ain't (have + be)* | 1.32 | (n.s.) | .83 | (n.s.) | 35.68 | .01[a] |
| Nonstandard irregular past participle | .72 | (n.s.) | .21 | (n.s.) | .10 | (n.s.) |
| Nonstandard irregular preterite | 6.62 | .05[a] | 3.89 | (n.s.) | 20.62 | .01[a] |

*Note:* Calculations are based on frequencies. n.s. = not significant. NP = noun phrase.
[a]Males more nonstandard. [b]Females more nonstandard.
*Source:* Feagin 1979:284.

for multiple negation. Also, according to table 3–5 a chi-square value above 3.841 at one degree of freedom gives a level of confidence of $p < .05$; several of her results listed in table 3–11 as not significant (n.s.) are indeed so.

Exclusive reliance on chi-square can lead to other difficulties. We noted that when the Detroit study gave a mean for a particular class, that mean was a function of total class behavior rather than of the results of a frequency distribution. Feagin's means are similar. As table 3–12 indi-

*Table 3–12.* Negative Concord within the Same Clause

| | Female | | | Male | |
|---|---|---|---|---|---|
| Informant | Occ./total | % | Informant | Occ./total | % |
| Upper-class children | | | | | |
| 9-EK | 3/11 | — | 23-KF | 0/15 | — |
| 9-AB | 0/8 | — | 23-HH | 0/11 | — |
| 1-BK | 0/18 | — | 24-TL | 0/8 | — |
| 13-DT | 0/9 | — | 24-SL | — | — |
| 13-BW | 1/8 | — | 20-BD | 0/32 | — |
| 12-LD | 0/10 | — | 25-JP | 0/15 | — |
| Total | 4/64 | 6.2 | Total | 0/81 | 0 |
| Upper-class adults | | | | | |
| 15-HH | 0/24 | — | 26-CW | 0/5 | — |
| 18-GC | 0/28 | — | 42-MH | 0/6 | — |
| 17-JG | 0/9 | — | 2-RK | 0/5 | — |
| 17-MG | 0/16 | — | 41-GB | 0/10 | — |
| 19-MV | 0/20 | — | 27-RD | 0/8 | — |
| 22-ED | 0/44 | — | 48-FO | 0/23 | — |
| Total | 0/141 | 0 | Total | 0/57 | 0 |
| Rural Working-class adults | | | | | |
| 11-MJ | 59/66 | — | 33-LN | 55/65 | — |
| 52-CR | 24/31 | — | 29-JH | 30/33 | — |
| 52-LS | 14/16 | — | 57-JM | 12/12 | — |
| 53-ET | 7/13 | — | 57-GR | 5/5 | — |
| 57-EM | 4/4 | — | 56-HF | 11/12 | — |
| 39-MH | 2/16 | — | 54-HC | 11/12 | — |
| 35-IM | 10/11 | — | 55-HB | 5/6 | — |
| 28-MD | 8/12 | — | — | — | — |
| Total | 128/169 | 75.7 | Total | 129/145 | 88.9 |

*Note:* Occ. = actual occurrences. Total = total possible occurrences.
*Source:* Feagin 1979:359.

cates, she took the total number of potential multiple negatives (negative concord) for each group as a whole and divided that number into the actual number of multiple negatives and hence arrived at the various means: 6.2 percent for the upper-class girls, 0 for the upper-class boys, 75.7 percent for the rural working-class women, and 88.9 percent for the rural working-class men. In this way, certain informants heavily influenced the results for their classes; that is, for the rural working-class women, informants MJ and CR represent much more than one-half of both the potential and the actual examples of multiple negation, and the same is true for LN and JH, rural working-class males. For this reason, it would have been better to set up a frequency distribution and to use a *t*-test, even though the results for some of the informants are meager indeed.

Table 3–13 illustrates the *t*-test for the rural working-class males and females. The fractions in table 3–12 have been converted into percen-

*Table 3–13.* Older Rural Informants: *t*-Test for Multiple Negation

| Frequencies (in percent) | |
|---|---|
| Women | Men |
| 1.  89.4 | 1.   84.6 |
| 2.  77.4 | 2.   90.9 |
| 3.  87.5 | 3. 100.0 |
| 4.  53.9 | 4. 100.0 |
| 5. 100.0 | 5.   91.7 |
| 6.  12.5 | 6.   91.7 |
| 7.  90.9 | 7.   83.3 |
| 8.  66.7 | — |

Note: $N_1 = 8$, $N_2 = 7$, $m_1 = 72.3$, $s_1 = 28.3$; $m_2 = 91.7$, $s_2 = 6.6$.

$$t = \frac{72.3 \ - \ 91.7}{\sqrt{\frac{7(28.3)^2 + 6(6.6)^2}{13}} \times \sqrt{\frac{1}{8} + \frac{1}{7}}}$$

$$= \frac{19.4}{11.0}$$

$$= 1.76$$

Therefore: since, for $p < .05$, at $df = 13$, $t$ must equal 2.160, the results (1.76) indicate that $p > .05$.

tages. The results here are not significant at $p < .05$; in fact, they are valid only at $p < .20$, according to table 3–1 ($df = 13$), so there is a 20 percent chance that Feagin's results are a function of her sample alone and not of the population which she is attempting to describe. In other words, the $t$-test contradicts the findings of chi-square because, in this case, the standard deviation for the women is extremely high. A $t$-test of the findings for the older urban working class (see table 3–14) demonstrates the same thing. The data are not from table 3–12. They come from another part of Feagin's book (1979:273). The standard deviations for both groups in table 3–14 are quite high, so the $t$-test yields a value of only .79 which, at ten degrees of freedom, gives a level of confidence of $p < .50$, or no confidence at all.

Although some of Feagin's conclusions are suspect because of certain mistakes in the use of chi-square, errors are not the rule. Moreover, we noted earlier that her results concerning black-white speech differences have gone a long way toward resolving the controversy which began in the mid-1960s, and those results put her squarely in the camp of scholars such as Labov and Wolfram. It seems appropriate to close this section

*Table 3–14.* Older Urban Informants: $t$-Test for Multiple Negation

| Frequencies (in percent) | |
| --- | --- |
| Women | Men |
| 1.    8 | 1.    0 |
| 2.    48 | 2.    0 |
| 3.    90 | 3.    73 |
| 4.    96 | 4.    74 |
| 5.  100 | 5.    83 |
| 6.  100 | 6.  100 |

*Note:* $N_1 = 6$, $N_2 = 6$, $m_1 = 73.7$, $s_1 = 37.7$, $m_2 = 55.0$, $s_2 = 43.7$.

$$t = \frac{73.7 \ - \ 55.0}{\sqrt{\dfrac{5(37.7)^2 \ + \ 5(43.7)^2}{10}} \times \sqrt{\dfrac{1}{6} + \dfrac{1}{6}}}$$

$$= \frac{18.7}{23.6}$$

$$= .79$$

Therefore: since, for $p < .05$, at $df = 10$, $t$ must equal 2.228, the results (.79) indicate that $p > .05$.

with a quotation from Wolfram (1971) written some eight years before Feagin reached the same conclusions:

> While we conclude that there are discrete Black-White speech differences in the South, we must also point out that the extent of these differences is not nearly as great as is sometimes claimed. Most of the differences are on a surface rather than on an underlying level of language organization. Claims about the drastic differences in the underlying structure of the verb phrase . . . simply cannot be validated on the basis of exhaustive descriptive analysis.
>
> It should be further pointed out that the inventory of differences is far smaller than the inventory of similarities. By focusing on the differences one may tend to overlook the many cases . . . in which these varieties of English are quite alike. One cannot, therefore, reason that we must assume significant identicalness unless evidence is proved to the contrary. [P. 156]

Wolfram's statement here is quite representative of the largest body of scholarly opinion regarding the identity of Black English. Differences between black speech and white do exist, and whereas most of them are quantitative in nature, a few qualitative differences can be found. These latter are not so much *which* forms are used but rather *how* the forms are used. There does not appear to be, in Black English, an underlying structure different from that in white speech. The historical question of the original creole remains open, but evidence suggests that one did in fact exist and that, moreover, some vestiges of it still remain in the speech of blacks in the lower social classes (see Rickford 1977 for a convincing statement of this position), but not enough to warrant the claims of the creolists. As so often happens in science, additional research on the English of black Americans is revealing that the truth tends to lie between two extreme positions.

The decade of the 1970s saw additional research on the English of black Americans. Many of the scholars involved in this research did not see themselves particularly as part of the Black English controversy; instead, they were interested in describing the English of blacks (and others) for its own sake. In so doing these workers began to talk of *variable rules,* and as we shall see, a discussion of variables rules properly belongs in a general framework of a discussion of structural dialectology.

## Other Social Dialects of American English

Although without question the major area of research for social dialectologists in the 1960s and 1970s was black speech, the middle years of the seventies did see the beginnings of interest in the language of whites in southern Appalachia. One work (L. M. Davis 1971) examined the speech of Appalachian in-migrants to Chicago, and others (Blanton 1974; McGreevy 1977) looked at various aspects of the grammatical system in Breathitt County, Kentucky; another study (Hackenberg 1973) also examined the sociolinguistic aspects of English in Appalachia. None of these studies has been published to date. Davis's 1971 work remains a report to the U.S. Office of Education, and the other three are unpublished doctoral dissertations. In fact, the only large-scale published study to date is that of Walt Wolfram and Donna Christian, *Appalachian Speech* (1976).

Wolfram and Christian tape-recorded the speech of 129 informants in two southern West Virginia counties: Mercer and Monroe. They then selected fifty-two informants for intensive study, pointing out that most of them "would be considered to be of the lower socio-economic level according to current indices, although there is some representation of the entire range of the population in this area" (1976:10). The study does not, however, list the informants in terms of their socioeconomic class.

The main social variables for the study are age and sex. There are four more females than males, so there are twenty-four males and twenty-eight females, divided into the following five age groups: seven to eleven, twelve to fourteen, fifteen to eighteen, twenty to forty, and over forty. Many of the results are based on the analysis of far fewer than fifty-two informants, however. Figure 3–10 presents the findings for multiple negation, based on twenty-five informants. In other cases, as in table 3–15, they use as few as thirteen informants, and in a few cases (consonant cluster reduction, p. 36) they use only six.

As table 3–15 indicates, Wolfram and Christian arrive at their means in the same way as did Shuy (1968) and Feagin (1979), and as we saw in our discussion of this method, it is far less reliable than a frequency distribution because any one informant can unduly influence the results for his class. In table 3–15, for example, we note that in each column certain informants were far more responsible for the totals than were others. Moreover, because the findings were not tested for significance, we have difficulty in interpreting statements such as the following, for utterances like *he's a-laughin'*:

> [Table 3–15] ... presents clear-cut support for the contention that *a*-prefixing is a phenomenon that is dying out in Appalachia. The eight speakers with the highest frequency levels for *a*-prefixing are all age 50 or older. Only three of the 13 speakers represented in the table are over age 30, and these three speakers all reveal *a*-prefixing at levels under 20 percent. [P. 74]

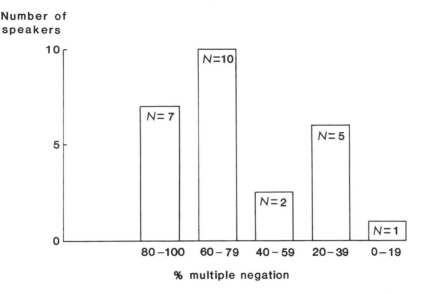

*Figure 3–10.* Distribution of Appalachian English Speakers with Respect to the Extent of Multiple Negation. *Source*: Wolfram and Christian 1976:10.

A *t*-test of these data supports the conclusions. In fact, the difference between the means of the first eight speakers in table 3–15 (29.87) and the last five (12.52) is valid at $p < .01$. On the other hand, only 25 percent of the total fifty-two informants are listed on the table, and all but four of the thirteen are male.

We noted above that the social variables which Wolfram and Christian correlate with linguistic variables are age and sex. No attention is given to the question of socioeconomic class, and one reason for this, it seems, is that Wolfram and Christian were interested in comparing the linguistic behavior of their Appalachian informants with that of other speakers in other studies. Table 3–16 presents one such comparison, having to do with consonant cluster reduction. While such comparisons are undoubtedly interesting, they shed little light on the question of social stratification of English in the Appalachian speech community. Blanton (1974), for example, found that the use of certain verb forms in Breathitt County, Kentucky, was a function of social class, which in turn was a function of whether an informant lived in town or in the rural area surrounding the town. In addition, because Wolfram and Christian included some informants of higher social status in their sample, the percentages for Appalachian speech in table 3–16 may be skewed downward a bit.

*Table 3–15.* A-Prefixing According to Grammatical Categories

| Informant no. | Age/Sex | Progressives No./total | % | Keep No./total | % | Movement verbs No./total | % | Adverbs No./total | % | Total No./total | % |
|---|---|---|---|---|---|---|---|---|---|---|---|
| 31 | 67/M | 13/28 | 53.6 | 0/2 | 0.0 | 2/3 | 66.7 | 2/7 | 28.6 | 17/40 | 42.5 |
| 83 | 93/M | 16/37 | 43.2 | 3/6 | 50.0 | 0/1 | 0.0 | 0/2 | 0.0 | 19/46 | 41.3 |
| 85 | 78/M | 16/57 | 31.6 | 4/4 | 100.0 | —/— | — | 3/12 | 25.0 | 25/73 | 34.2 |
| 153 | 83/F | 9/35 | 25.7 | 0/1 | 0.0 | 2/2 | 100.0 | 1/4 | 25.0 | 12/42 | 28.6 |
| 22 | 60/M | 18/64 | 28.1 | —/— | — | 0/4 | 0.0 | 3/11 | 27.3 | 21/79 | 26.6 |
| 152 | 64/F | 11/43 | 25.6 | 1/4 | 25.0 | 1/1 | 100.0 | 1/10 | 10.0 | 14/58 | 24.1 |
| 157 | 52/F | 14/52 | 26.9 | —/— | — | 0/3 | 0.0 | 1/8 | 12.5 | 15/63 | 23.8 |
| 30 | 50/M | 7/52 | 13.5 | 1/5 | 20.0 | 2/5 | 40.0 | 4/16 | 25.0 | 14/78 | 17.9 |
| 44 | 14/M | 4/41 | 9.7 | 1/2 | 50.0 | 4/7 | 57.1 | 0/3 | 0.0 | 9/53 | 17.0 |
| 124 | 11/M | 1/45 | 2.2 | 1/2 | 50.0 | 8/16 | 50.0 | 0/10 | 0.0 | 10/73 | 13.7 |
| 146 | 52/M | 9/59 | 15.3 | —/— | — | 0/10 | 0.0 | 0/9 | 0.0 | 9/78 | 11.5 |
| 2 | 13/M | 3/54 | 5.6 | 5/13 | 38.5 | 1/12 | 8.3 | 0/5 | 0.0 | 9/84 | 10.7 |
| 29 | 33/F | 7/79 | 8.9 | —/— | — | 1/10 | 10.0 | 1/4 | 25.0 | 9/93 | 9.7 |
| Totals | — | 130/646 | 20.1 | 16/39 | 41.0 | 21/74 | 28.4 | 16/101 | 15.8 | 183/860 | 21.3 |

*Note:* No. = actual number of occurrences of a-prefixing. Total = total number of possible occurrences.
*Source:* Wolfram and Christian 1976:75.

## *Table 3–16.* Comparison of Consonant Cluster Varieties

| | Percentage of simplified consonant clusters | | | |
|---|---|---|---|---|
| Language variety | Not *-ed,* followed by consonant | *-ed* Followed by consonant | Not *-ed,* followed by vowel | *-ed* Followed by vowel |
| Middle-class white Detroit speech | 66 | 36 | 12 | 3 |
| Working-class black Detroit speech | 97 | 76 | 72 | 34 |
| Working-class white New York City Adolescent speech | 67 | 23 | 19 | 3 |
| Working-class white Adolescent rural Georgia-Florida speech | 56 | 16 | 25 | 10 |
| Working-class black Adolescent, rural Georgia-Florida speech | 88 | 50 | 72 | 36 |
| Southeastern West Virginia speech | 74 | 67 | 17 | 5 |

*Source:* Wolfram and Christian 1976:36.
*Note: -ed* = past or past participial suffix.

Another question raised by *Appalachian Speech* concerns the matter of the definition of standard English. Although Wolfram and Christian do note early in the book (1976:29–31) that spoken standard English is relative, depending on the area of the United States in question, their actual use of the term is more simplistic. That is, unlike Feagin (1979), who included upper-class speakers for comparison, Wolfram and Christian decided not to do so. "Southern White Varieties" in table 3–17 refers to speakers in rural Georgia, which are not the basis for the best kinds of comparisons.

Clearly much more research is needed in the area of Appalachian English, in all its varieties, since there is clearly dialectal variation within the Appalachian region. Hackenberg (1973), Blanton (1974), and McGreevy (1977) have provided a beginning, but none of these studies has been published in full. Wolfram and Christian added to our knowledge, but their work does suffer from the lack of socioeconomic data and from its lack of information on the standard English of Mercer and

*Table 3–17.* Different Types of Negation in Various Dialects of English

| English dialect | Postverbal indefinites | Preverbal indefinite/ negative auxiliary | Negative inversion | Negative auxiliary across clauses |
|---|---|---|---|---|
| Standard English | 0 | 0 | 0 | 0 |
| Some northern white varieties | X | 0 | 0 | 0 |
| Other northern white varieties | X | X | 0 | 0 |
| Some southern white varieties | X | X | X | 0 |
| Appalachian English | X | X | X | X |
| Vernacular Black English | 1 | X | X | X |

*Source:* Wolfram and Christian 1976:115.

Monroe counties. But at least a start has been made in the attempt to understand linguistic variation in southern Appalachia.

When we turn to other social dialects of American English, however, the situation is less encouraging. Wolfram (1974b) has examined the English of Puerto Ricans in New York City, and Leap (1974) made a start in the area of the English of native Americans, but much is left to be done in those areas and in others, such as Chicano English. Not surprisingly, given the political and social situation in the United States in the past two decades, most of the research has centered on the language of black Americans.

In the next chapter, rather than concentrating on the conclusions of various studies, we shall examine the question of method—of how to present results. Because the 1970s saw linguists trying to grapple with new kinds of data, their models for linguistic description changed, and the related questions of structural dialectology and variable rules became central. As linguists began to realize that linguistic behavior is inconsistent and variable but at the same time predictable, it became important to find linguistic models which adequately describe that variation. Hence structural dialectology, and hence chapter 4 of this book.

# 4

# *The Search for a Structural Dialectology*

In the brief survey of the history of linguistic geography in chapter 2, we saw that the discipline had its beginnings in Europe during the last century and that, in essence, methods of analysis have not changed significantly since that period. That is, the task of the dialect geographer was, and still is, to draw isoglosses which isolate different pronunciations, grammatical usages, and lexical variants. From their outset, with the exception of the Scottish atlas, all linguistic atlases published to date have been basically word centered; the question asked about pronunciation, for example, has always been, "How do different speakers pronounce a certain word?" be that word *grease, greasy,* or whatever. To be sure, the variant pronunciations of *Mary, merry,* and *marry* do carry phonological information, but even the *LAUM,* the most recent American atlas, presents results in terms of the ways in which the informants pronounce various words. Similarly, in the field of word geography, the dialect geographer has historically tried to find different words for the same thing or phenomenon—the dragonfly, *left-handed,* and so on.

When we take into account that the major European atlases and the *LANE* were all planned before 1930, we should understand that this development preceded the movement in the study of language known as *structuralism,* the prime mover of which, in North America at least, was Leonard Bloomfield. Bloomfield's classic text, *Language,* appeared in 1933, when the phoneme had already been recognized as a basic element in linguistic analysis. In fact, Bloomfield argued that the only important elements at the phonological level are phonemes and that subphonemic variation is far less worthy of linguistic study. Bloomfield's chapter on dialectology was quite historical in perspective, stressing phonemic differences existing between dialects.

These two approaches to dialect variation—the structuralist's and the dialect geographer's—seem to be irreconcilable. In the *greassy-greazy* example, a speaker who says the former will most certainly say *sleazy*, so he or she does have /z/ intervocalically; both /s/ and /z/ are phonemes in the person's speech, so at the phonemic level there are no differences between *greassy* speakers and *greazy* speakers, based on that evidence alone. The two groups differ, in this case, only in the incidence of sounds in a certain word, so drawing a *greassy-greazy* isogloss says little to the structuralist concerning the linguistic systems of the dialects in question.

This conflict between structuralism and dialect geography was noted quite frequently during the first half of this century, but nowhere was it more succinctly described than in the opening paragraphs of Uriel Weinreich's article, "Is a Structural Dialectology Possible?" (1954, quoted from Allen and Underwood 1971):

> In linguistics today the abyss between structural and dialectological studies appears greater than it ever was. . . . Students continue to be trained in one domain at the expense of the other. . . . The stauncher adherents of each discipline claim priority for their own method and charge the others with "impressionism" and "metaphysics," as the case may be; the more pliant are prepared to concede that they are simply studying different aspects of the same reality.
>
> This might seem like a welcome truce in an old controversy, but is it an honorable truce? A compromise induced by fatigue cannot in the long run be satisfactory to either party. The controversy could be resolved only if the structuralists as well as the dialectologists found a reasoned place for the other discipline in their theory of language. But for the disciplines to legitimate each other is tantamount to establishing a unified theory of language on which both of them could operate. This has not yet been done. [P. 300]

Weinreich went on to set up some general principles for a structural dialectology. For example, he suggested that the traditional dialectological approach to phonological, grammatical, and lexical differences could be modified to make it more in line with structuralist principles.

For phonology, Weinreich used the example (here simplified somewhat) of speakers who pronounce the word *man* in the following ways: (1) [man], (2) [man], (3) [mæn]. The traditional dialectological approach would obviously put speakers 1 and 2 together in one dialect and speaker 3 in another, but according to Weinreich's structuralist approach, this may not be the best solution to the problem. Suppose, he argues, that speaker 1 speaks a dialect where vowel length is significant, whereas speakers 2 and 3 do not. In that case, the phonemic transcription for informant 1's pronunciaton would be /măn/, as opposed to informant 2's /man/. Similarly, it is conceivable that the [æ] of informant 3 occurs only between nasals and thus is a positional variant of /a/. In this situation, the correct phonemic transcription of 3's pronunciation of *man* is /man/, as it was for informant 2. So on the basis of these hypothetical data only, it makes sense to group speakers 2 and 3 together and to put speaker 1 in a different dialect.

Weinreich gave other examples in the areas of morphology and lexicon. He pointed out that Eastern European Yiddish has the word *shtul*, but that the word means different things in different dialects. In one dialect it means "easy chair," and in another simply "chair," so the typical nonstructural dialectologist's map would look something like figure 4–1. The structural dialectologist, on the other hand, approaches this problem differently. First of all, it is clear that the speakers of dialect A here do have some word for an easy chair, and that speakers of dialect B have a word for an ordinary chair. For that reason, says Weinreich, it is worth delving deeper than is usually done in word geography. If one would find, for example, that both dialects have the word *benkl* and that it means "little bench" in dialect A and "seat" in B and that speakers of A use the word *fotél* for "easy chair," then one could draw the map in figure 4–2 showing the relationships between the various words.

Weinreich closed his article with considerable optimism. He believed in structural dialectology, and since his pioneering paper, several scholars have attempted to apply Weinreich's theory. One of the first to do so was Robert P. Stockwell in "Structural Dialectology: A Proposal" (1959).

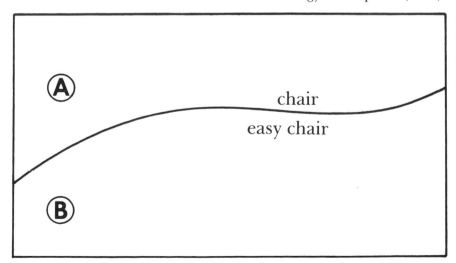

*Figure 4–1*. Nonstructural Dialectologist's Map: *Chair* and *Easy Chair*. *Source*: Adapted from Weinreich 1954:398.

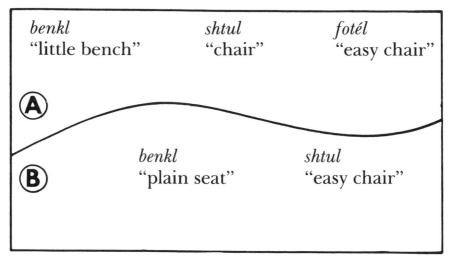

*Figure 4–2.* Structural Dialectologist's Map: *Benkl, Shtul,* and *Fotél. Source:* Weinreich 1954:398.

Stockwell proposed using the analysis of Trager and Smith (1951) to map different dialects into their component phonemes, or, to use Weinreich's term, *diaphonemes.* Stockwell's notion, however, never went beyond the proposal stage and was never actually implemented using linguistic data gathered in fieldwork.

The main impulse toward a structural dialectology came at the same time that traditional linguistic theory itself was undergoing a challenge, with the development of generative grammar and the search for language universals. Generative grammarians gave some attention to dialects, but admittedly dialectology never was central to the theory; they were concerned more with the competence of ideal speaker-listeners in a homogeneous speech community than with the performance of actual informants. Phonology, however, is considered performance by generative linguistics, and it was Morris Halle who first suggested that problems in dialectology could be solved with the ordering and reordering of phonological rules.

In "Phonology and Generative Grammar" (1962), Halle suggested that two dialects of Canadian English can be shown to be related by the ordering of two rules, simplified somewhat here. He took his example from Joos (1942), where the two dialects in question are differentiated by the pronunciation of the word *typewriter.* Dialect A has [tɛɪprɛɪdɚ], and B has [tɛɪpraɪdɚ]. The two rules proposed by Halle are the following: (1) [a] becomes [ɐ] in diphthongs followed by voiceless consonants and (2) [t] becomes [d] intervocalically. The underlying form, the input to the rule, which Halle set up is [taɪpraɪtɚ]. If we take the underlying form and apply first rule 1 and then rule 2, we have the following:

| | |
|---|---|
| Underlying form: | taɪpraɪtɚ |
| Rule 1: | tɐɪprɐɪtɚ |
| Rule 2: | tɐɪprɐɪdɚ (Dialect A) |

If, on the other hand, we apply rule 2 and then rule 1, we get the pronunciation of *typewriter* in dialect B:

| | |
|---|---|
| Underlying form: | taɪpraɪtɚ |
| Rule 2: | taɪpraɪdɚ |
| Rule 1: | tɐɪpraɪdɚ (Dialect B) |

In this second example, rule 1, which turns [a] into [ɐ] in diphthongs before voiceless stops, does not apply to the second syllable because rule 2 has already changed [t], the voiceless stop in the underlying form, to [d], which is voiced. The ordering of rules, quite common in much of today's generative phonology, accounts for the relationship between these two Canadian dialects.

This idea was carried still further by Samuel J. Keyser, in his 1963 review of Kurath's and McDavid's *Pronunciation of English in the Atlantic States (PEAS)* (1961). According to Keyser, many of the relationships between the dialects in *PEAS* were unstated by the authors because Kurath and McDavid did not use generative rules. One of the problems with Keyser's analysis, however, was noted orally by Lee A. Pederson in 1964, who observed that Keyser had simplified the *PEAS* data in several cases. Since the review is frequently cited by scholars and was recently characterized by Labov (quoted in Feagin 1979:ix) as a "provocative inquiry into the questions that might be answered . . . by rule ordering," it seems wise to examine Keyser's review in some detail here. He first presents *PEAS* data, simplified somewhat, from three informants: from Winchester, Virginia, Charleston, South Carolina, and New Bern, North Carolina:

*Winchester*

| | | | | |
|---|---|---|---|---|
| five | ɑ·ɛ | down | æ·u |
| twice | ɐ ɨ | out | ɐu |

*Charleston*

| | | | | |
|---|---|---|---|---|
| five | ɑ·ɨ | down | au |
| twice | ɐ ɨ | out | ɐ u |

*New Bern*

| | | | | |
|---|---|---|---|---|
| five | ɑ·ɛ | down | æ·u |
| twice | ɑ·ɛ | out | æu |

Then he gives the following two phonological rules:

1. a → ɐ before a vowel followed by a voiceless consonant
2. a → æ before u

The underlying form for the vowel in all four words is [a].

Charleston can be described, according to Keyser, by rule 1 only, so *five* and *down* are unaffected. In *twice* and *out*, the vowels become [ɐ]. New Bern, on the other hand, can be described by rule 2 only, so we get [æ] in *down* and *out*, but *twice* and *five* remain unaffected. Winchester is still different, since two ordered rules are required to describe it. First rule 1 changes the vowels in *twice* and *out* to [ɐ]. Then rule 2 applies, changing the vowel in *down* to [æ]. Note that *out* remains unaffected by the application of rule 2 here because rule 1 had previously changed its vowel to [ɐ], and rule 2 applies only to cases of [a].

Keyser goes on to suggest how the two rules might have spread and argues that his formulation of rules is much simpler than the approach in *PEAS*:

> By ordering our rules, we have been able to simplify our description of a given dialect. We have seen, moreover, that through a comparison of rules and their respective orderings from one dialect to another, the possibility now arises of accounting for the formation of new dialect groups through the geographical dissemination of rules. [P. 313]

The approach does indeed look neat, but the fact is that Keyser's rules do not describe enough of what really is going on in the dialects in question. For example, the New Bern informant differs from the other two in the pronunciation of *five* and from the Charleston informant in the pronunciation of *twice*; although Kurath and McDavid note that this lower off-glide is frequently significant in differentiating American dialects, this difference is not generated by Keyser's rules. Moreover, a glance at the data reveals four different sorts of *a*: [a], [ɐ], [æ], [ɑ]; yet only the first three of them are generated by the rules. It is as though [a] and [ɑ] were the same. It can also be noted that only the Charleston informant has a short onset for the diphthong in *down* (there is no dot after the first vowel in the diphthong). Kurath and McDavid make the point (1961:109) that this is a significant differentiating feature, but it cannot be generated by Keyser's rules.

The rules do work, as far as they go, but they fall far short of describing the major differences between the three informants because they ignore too much phonetic detail. Although Kurath and McDavid point to places in the United States where *house* and *out* are pronounced with [əu], as opposed to areas where these words are pronounced with [ɐu], these are treated as the same sound in Keyser's rule 1 ([ɐ]). In short, the rules describe only part of the trends in the data, and there is no way even to know if that which the rules describe is in fact more significant than that which they do not.

Another step forward in structural dialectology based on a generative model was that taken by Rudolph Troike in his "Overall Pattern and Generative Phonology" (1971). Troike set up underlying diaphonemes and showed that certain orderings of rules, and in some cases different rules altogether, can explain the relationships between a number of British and American dialects. Troike argued that all English dialects have an underlying diaphonemic system and that one of the major tasks of the dialectologist is to discover the rules which convert these underlying forms into the phonetic reality for each English dialect. His approach was a distinct advance over that of James Sledd (1966), who used generative rules to describe his own Atlanta idiolect.

But the generative approach had serious drawbacks, mainly because it provides no system for expressing linguistic diversity even in the speech of a single individual. Sledd (1966), for example, described his own speech as if it were totally consistent, whereas Labov and others had shown that linguistic behavior is sometimes inconsistent indeed (see chapter 3). We saw in the last chapter that linguistic theory was affected profoundly by these discoveries, and hence new models were introduced to account for such variability. It is worth noting here that none of the models that we have examined thus far takes full enough account of this variability. Weinreich's *man* example tends to assume that informant 1's pronunciation is always [man], whereas in fact it just might be that plus a whole lot of nonphonemic variants. L. M. Davis (1973) listed the transcriptions shown in figure 4–3, recorded as variants of the phoneme /i/, in words like *peach*.

It seems clear enough that some method of analysis must be able to handle such variation and describe it systematically. Davis (1973) sug-

*Figure 4–3.* Transcribed Variants of the Phoneme /i/. *Source*: L. M. Davis 1973:7.

gested a *diafeature* analysis, whereby underlying forms could be mapped into a larger grid which would provide ranges of permitted variation for any dialect in question. This grid was based on the system of transcription used in articulatory phonetics. A vowel can be written simply [V] or with shift signs: [V^] raising, [Vˇ] lowering. These, of course, can be combined, so that [V^>] is a vowel which is both raised and backed from its typical position. These shift signs are exemplified in the transcriptions in figure 4–3. The grid for the underlying diaphoneme /i/ appears as figure 4–4. A transcription such as [i^>] would then receive a high value of 1 and a back value of 3, and if we were to work through all of the transcriptions in figure 4–3 in this way, we would find that they have the ranges shown in figure 4–5.

Other features are also presented in Davis (1973), and for the most part that system does provide a means to describe not only idiolectal variation but dialectal variation as well. For example, it was suggested (L. M. Davis 1976) that the ranges for the various diaphonemes for any one speaker were the same as those for all the speakers of the same dialect; hence, as Weinreich had hoped, there is now a way to determine objectively whether two speakers belong phonologically to the same or to different dialects. The major problem with the diafeature system, however, was that it did not adequately take into account the question of

| High values \ Back values | 1 | 2 | 3 | 4 | 5 | 6 |
|---|---|---|---|---|---|---|
| 1 | | | | | | |
| 2 | | i | | | ɨ | |
| 3 | | | | | | |
| 4 | | | | | | |
| 5 | | ɪ | | | ᵻ | |
| 6 | | | | | | |

*Figure 4–4.* Diafeature Analysis of the Diaphoneme /i/. *Source*: L. M. Davis 1973:5.

| | 1 | 2 |
|---|---|---|
| /i/ → | 2–5 back<br>2–5 high<br>5 round<br>1 long<br>2 nasal | 2–5 back<br>1–3 high<br>5 round<br>1 long<br>2 nasal |

*Figure 4–5.* Diafeature Analysis of Transcribed Variants of the Phoneme /i/. *Source*: L. M. Davis 1973:7.

variation as a function of style and social class. That is, many of the transcriptions in figure 4–3 might be a function of one or both of these and, given Davis's system, there is no way to know. Moreover, the model as presented is static and does not provide any means for determining which ranges and which diaphonemes are socially significant.

The question of how to describe masses of data has never been solved satisfactorily. Progress has been made, however, in another area of linguistic analysis where the problems of description are different, though no less complex. We noted that Labov and those who followed him discovered that certain cases of apparent free variation were in fact predictable, so one of the problems of the 1970s was to determine just how to formulate such rules, rules which are *optional* in a very special sense.

To understand this problem, one must first understand the distinction between optional and obligatory rules. Wolfram and Fasold (1974) point out that an obligatory rule in phonology would be the aspiration of voiceless stops at the beginnings of words. An optional rule, on the other hand, would be the deletion of the final stop in the expression *east precincts*. Sometimes people just do not pronounce the /t/ in *east*; at other times they do. In addition, linguists have found that the presence of a following vowel greatly reduces the probability of consonant cluster reduction, so people are less likely to "drop the /t/" in an expression like *east end*; it is actually possible, then, to set up a hierarchy of such rules.

Beginning with Labov's (1969) study of black speech and continuing to the present time, much effort has been expended in developing socalled variable rules. The various environments in which variable rules operate are called *constraints*. A typical rule might be that shown below, for the reduction of consonant clusters. It is adapted from Wolfram and Fasold (1974:116).

$$C_{st} \rightarrow (\emptyset) \; / \; _B C_{(son)} \underline{\hspace{2cm}} \#\# \sim_A (V)$$

The rule says that a stop consonant ($C_{st}$) becomes ($\rightarrow$) deleted ($\emptyset$) in the environment of (/) a following word boundary ($\#\#$). The $C_{(son)}$ means that there can be an optional sonorant (nasal or /l/) and the $\sim$-(V) means "when there is not a vowel (in the next word)." The letters A and B describe the variable constraints and indicate that the absence of a vowel in the following word is more "important," ranked higher, than the sonorant which precedes the cluster in question.

Actual variable rules are usually expressed in distinctive features (see Schane 1973 for an introduction to this subject), but however they are expressed, they indicate which optional rules apply and in what linguistic environments. Cedergren and Sankoff (1974) have taken this approach still further, producing a probabilistic model and computer program for predicting the operation of certain variable constraints, and Rousseau and Sankoff (1978) have revised that model to some extent. A description of how the model actually works is beyond the range of this book. It is important to note here that particularly in the last half of the 1970s, considerable progress was made in the formulation of variable rules.

In the quotation of Weinreich (1954) above, we noted that he called for "a unified theory of language" which could unify the structuralist and the dialectological positions. The linguists who have engaged in developing variable rules clearly see generative grammar as that theory. It should be clear to the reader familiar with generative grammar that such rules are special in kind—optional and dialect specific. If we take the position of Rousseau and Sankoff (1978) to its logical conclusion, then each dialect must have its own predicted probabilities for each variable rule. Of course, the qualitative nature of variable rules will also depend on the dialect in question; a rule which deletes forms of the verb *be*, for example, is needed for certain dialects of Black English but surely not for upper-class Chicago speech.

It seems best to view the question of variable rules, as we have done, in the context of structural dialectology. In one sense, they are a distinct improvement over the early generative approaches (Halle 1962, Sledd 1966, Troike 1971), mainly because they deal with real data from large numbers of informants and are based on actual fieldwork. In another sense, however, they are less adequate, because they deal only with points in a linguistic system rather than with the system as a whole. Troike (1971), on the other hand, tried to set up diaphonemes which could be the basis for rewrite rules mapping underlying forms into surface realities throughout the system. We noted that his approach does not handle linguistic inconsistency, something easily describable using variable rules. To date, however, no linguist has developed a system of variable rules for any one entire system of a dialect, be that system phonological, grammatical, or lexical.

L. M. Davis's (1973) formulation, using ranges, is essentially the Troike system with the added feature that it describes free variation. We have already discussed its weaknesses, observing that it is not sociolinguistically sensitive. Another weakness, perhaps more important in fact, is that it is useful for phonology only. Variable rules, of course, are formulated so as to be descriptive of phonological and grammatical phenomena as well, though they lack the ability to function systemwide; instead, they describe certain variations from standard English norms, although these norms themselves are never the product of actual analysis.

Moreover, we are still far from answering another question posed by Weinreich (1954). We have no adequate linguistic model which permits us to determine whether two idiolects belong to the same or to different dialects. L. M. Davis (1976) suggested that the only theory used by dialectologists in this area is "apparent similarity," so that when two idiolects "seem the same," then we say that they are so. Although Bailey (1973) has made some progress in this area, no one has dealt adequately with the problem of how to quantify two idiolects so as to say that they belong to the same or to different dialects. A. L. Davis (1972b) once proposed a *system of systems* approach, but unfortunately the idea was never fully developed, nor was it published even in preliminary form. The question is still open, and until this basic problem is solved, we remain far from a unified theory of dialectology.

Although significant progress was made in the 1970s, that decade left us far short of the goal set by Weinreich. A. L. Davis once observed orally that in some senses Weinreich posed the wrong question. The question, said Davis, is not whether a structural dialectology is possible but rather whether structural linguistics is possible without structural dialectology. Anshen (1978:2) has pointed out that "the supply of ideal speaker-listeners has been radically depleted in recent years." Surely one of the tasks of dialectologists in the 1980s and beyond is to formulate a model which is descriptively adequate, which can be used to describe the actual performance of people, even if people are so inconsiderate as to make rule writing difficult.

The task is far from completed, and this chapter is quite brief. It is to be hoped that future linguists will add sufficiently to our knowledge, so that instead of a short chapter, someone will be able to write a long book on the subject of structural dialectology.

# Bibliography

Allen, Harold B. 1973–76. *The Linguistic Atlas of the Upper Midwest.* 3 vols. (1973, 1975, 1976). Minneapolis: University of Minnesota Press.

———, and Underwood, Gary. 1971. *Readings in American Dialectology.* New York: Merideth.

Anshen, Frank. 1978. *Statistics for Linguists.* Rowley, Mass.: Newbury House.

Atwood, E. Bagby. 1950. "Grease and Greasy: A Study of Geographical Variation." *University of Texas Studies in English* 29:249–60.

———. 1953. *A Survey of Verb Forms in the Eastern United States.* Ann Arbor: University of Michigan Press.

Bailey, Beryl Loftman. 1965. "Toward a New Perspective in Negro English Dialectology." *American Speech* 40:171–77. Reprinted in Wolfram and Clarke 1971:41–50.

Bailey, Charles-James N. 1973. *Variation and Linguistic Theory.* Washington, D.C.: Center for Applied Linguistics.

Bennett, John. 1908. "Gullah: A Negro Patois." *South Atlantic Quarterly* 7:332–47.

Billiard, Charles E., and Pederson, Lee. 1979. "Composition of the LAGS Urban Complement: Atlanta Words." *Orbis* 26:223–41.

Blanton, Lindon Lonon. 1974. "The Verb System in Breathitt County, Kentucky: A Sociolinguistic Analysis." Ph.D. Dissertation, Illinois Institute of Technology.

Bloomfield, Leonard. 1933. *Language.* New York: Holt, Rinehart and Winston.

Cedergren, Henrietta, and Sankoff, David. 1974. "Variable Rules: Performance as a Statistical Reflection of Competence." *Language* 50:333–55.

Chomsky, Noam. 1965. *Aspects of the Theory of Syntax.* Cambridge, Mass.: MIT Press.

Davis, A. L. 1948. "A Word Atlas of the Great Lakes Region." Ph.D. Dissertation, University of Michigan.

———. 1972a. *Culture, Class, and Language Variety.* Urbana: National Council of Teachers of English.

———. 1972b. "Allophonic Analysis in Dialectology." Paper presented at the First International Conference on Methods in Dialectology, Charlottetown, Prince Edward Island. July.

Davis, Lawrence M. 1971. *A Study of Appalachian Speech in a Northern Urban Setting.* Project No. O-E-142. Chicago: U.S. Office of Education.

———. 1973. "The Diafeature: An Approach to Structural Dialectology." *Journal of English Linguistics* 7:1–20.

———. 1976. "Dialectology and Linguistics." *Orbis* 26:24–30.

Dillard, J. L. 1972. *Black English: Its History and Usage in the United States.* New York: Random House.

———. 1975. *All-American English.* New York: Random House.

Ellis, Alexander J. 1869–89. *On Early English Pronunciation.* London: Early English Text Society.

Fasold, Ralph. 1972. *Tense Marking in Black English: A Linguistic and Social Analysis.* Washington, D.C.: Center for Applied Linguistics.

Feagin, Crawford. 1979. *Variation and Change in Alabama English: A Sociolinguistic Study of the White Community.* Washington, D.C.: Georgetown University Press.

Fisher, Ronald A. 1970. *Statistical Methods for Research Workers*. 14th ed. Adelaide, South Australia: University of Adelaide.

Fishman, Joshua A., ed. 1970. *Readings in the Sociology of Language*. The Hague: Mouton.

Gilliéron, Jules. 1902–10. *Atlas linguistique de la France*. 13 vols. Paris: Champion.

Grose, Francis. 1785. *Classical Dictionary of the Vulgar Tongue*. London: S. Hooper.

———. 1787. *Provincial Glossary, with a Collection of Local Proverbs and Popular Superstitions*. London: n.p.

Hackenberg, Robert. 1973. "A Sociolinguistic Description of Appalachian English." Ph.D. Dissertation, Georgetown University.

Hall, Edward T. 1959. *The Silent Language*. Garden City, N.Y.: Doubleday.

———. 1966. *The Hidden Dimension*. Garden City, N.Y.: Doubleday.

Halle, Morris. 1962. "Phonology in Generative Grammar." *Word* 18:54–72. Reprinted in *The Structure of Language: Readings in the Philosophy of Language*, ed. J. A. Fodor and J. J. Katz, pp. 334–52. Englewood Cliffs, N.J.: Prentice-Hall, 1964.

Hollingshead, August de Belmont, and Redlich, Frederick C. 1958. *Social Class and Mental Illness*. New York: John Wiley.

Hubbell, Allen F. 1950. *The Pronunciation of English in New York City: Consonants and Vowels*. New York: Kings Crown Press.

Jaberg, Karl, and Jud, Jakob. 1928–40. *Sprach- und Sachatlas des Italiens und der Südschweiz*. Zofingen: Ringier.

Joos, Martin. 1942. "A Phonological Dilemma in Canadian English." *Language* 18:141–44.

Keyser, Samuel J. 1963. Review of Kurath and McDavid 1961. *Language* 39:303–16.

Kolb, Eduard. 1964. *Phonological Atlas of the Northern Region: The Six Northern Counties, North Lincolnshire, and the Isle of Man*. Bern: Franke Verlag.

———. 1979. *Atlas of English Sounds*. Bern: Franke Verlag.

Krapp, George Phillip. 1924. "The English of the Negro." *American Mercury* 2:190–95.

Kurath, Hans. 1949. *A Word Geography of the Eastern United States*. Ann Arbor: University of Michigan Press.

———. 1968. "The Investigation of Urban Speech." *Publication of the American Dialect Society* 49:1–7.

———, and McDavid, Raven I., Jr. 1961. *The Pronunciation of English in the Atlantic States*. Ann Arbor: University of Michigan Press.

———, et al. 1939. *Handbook of the Linguistic Georgraphy of New England*. Providence, R. I.: Brown University Press.

———, et al. 1939–43. *The Linguistic Atlas of New England*. Providence, R.I.: Brown University Press.

Labov, William. 1966. *The Social Stratification of English in New York City*. Washington, D.C.: Center for Applied Linguistics.

———. 1969. "Contraction, Deletion, and Inherent Variability of the English Copula." *Language* 45:715–62.

———. 1972. *Language in the Inner City: Studies in the Black English Vernacular*. Philadelphia: University of Pennsylvania Press.

———, et al. 1968. *A Study of the Non-Standard English of Negro and Puerto Rican Speakers in New York City*. Cooperative Research Project No. 3288. Washington, D.C.: U.S. Office of Education.

Leap, William L. 1972. "On Grammaticality in Native American English: The Evidence from Isleta." *Linguistics* 128:79–89.

McDavid, Raven I., Jr. 1948. "Postvocalic /r/ in South Carolina: A Social Analysis." *American Speech* 23:194–203.

———. 1958. "The Dialects of American English." In W. N. Francis, *The Structure of American English*, pp. 480–533. New York: Ronald Press.

———. 1966. "Sense and Nonsense about American Dialects." *Publications of the Modern Language Association* 81:7–17. Reprinted in Allen and Underwood 1971:36–52.

———. 1971. "Two Studies of Dialects of English." *Leeds Studies in English* 2:29–34.

———. 1972. "Field Procedures for Investigators, Linguistic Atlas of the Gulf States." In *A Manual for Dialect Research in the Southern States*, ed. Lee A. Pederson et al., pp. 35–60. Atlanta: Georgia State University Press.

———, and Davis, Lawrence M. 1972. "The Speech of Negro Americans." In *Studies in Linguistics in Honor of George L. Trager*, ed. M. E. Smith, pp. 303–12. The Hague: Mouton.

———, and McDavid, Virginia Glenn. 1951. "The Relationship of the Speech of American Negroes to the Speech of Whites." *American Speech* 26:3–17. Reprinted in Wolfram and Clarke 1971:16–40.

McGreevy, John C. 1977. "Breathitt County, Kentucky, Grammar." Ph.D. Dissertation, Illinois Institute of Technology.

McIntosh, Angus. 1952. *Introduction to a Survey of Scottish Dialects*. Edinburgh and London: Thomas Nelson and Sons.

Marckwardt, Albert H. 1957. "Principal and Subsidiary Dialect Areas in the North-Central States." *Publication of the American Dialect Society* 27:3–15. Reprinted in Allen and Underwood 1971:74–82.

Mather, J. Y., and Speitel, H. H. 1975, 1977. *Linguistic Atlas of Scotland*. 2 vols. London: Croom Helm.

Meillet, Antoine. 1906. "L'état actuel des études de linguistique générale." In *Linguistique historique et linguistique générale*, pp. 1–18. Paris: Champion, 1965.

Mencken, H. L. 1963. *The American Language*, ed. Raven I. McDavid, Jr. New York: Alfred A. Knopf.

Moulton, William. 1972. "Geographical Linguistics." In *Current Trends in Linguistics*, vol. 9, ed. Thomas A. Sebeok, pp. 186–222. The Hague: Mouton.

Orton, Harold. 1933. *The Phonology of a South Durham Dialect*. London: K. Paul, Trench, Trubner.

———. 1960. "An English Dialect Survey: Linguistic Atlas of England." *Orbis* 9:331–48. Reprinted in Allen and Underwood 1971:230–44.

———. 1962. *Survey of English Dialects: Introduction*. Leeds: E. J. Arnold and Son.

———, et al. 1962–71. *Survey of English Dialects: Basic Material*. 4 vols. Leeds: E. J. Arnold and Son.

———, Sanderson, Stewart, and Widdowson, John. 1978. *Linguistic Atlas of England*. London: Croom Helm.

———, and Wright, Nathalia. 1974. *A Word Geography of England*. London: Seminar Press.

Pederson, Lee A. 1964. "The Pronunciation of English in Metropolitan Chicago: Consonants and Vowels." Ph.D. Dissertation, University of Chicago.

Pickford, Glenna R. 1956. "American Linguistic Geography: A Sociological Appraisal." *Word* 12:211–33.

Pop, Sever. 1950. *La dialectologie.* 2 vols. Louvain: Centre Internationale de Dialectologie Générale.

Rickford, John. 1977. "The Question of Prior Creolization in Black English." In *Pidgin and Creole Linguistics*, ed. A. Valdman, pp. 190–220. Bloomington: Indiana University Press.

Rousseau, Pascale, and Sankoff, David. 1978. "Advances in Variable Rule Methodology." In *Linguistic Variation: Models and Methods*, ed. David Sankoff, pp. 57–69. New York and London: Academic Press.

Sapir, Edward. 1921. *Language.* New York: Harcourt, Brace and World.

———. 1931. "Dialect." In *Encyclopaedia of the Social Sciences*, vol. 5, ed. E. R. A. Seligman, pp. 123–26. New York: Macmillan.

Schane, Sanford. 1973. *Generative Phonology.* Englewood Cliffs, N.J.: Prentice-Hall.

Shuy, Roger W. 1968. *A Study of Social Dialects in Detroit.* Project No. 6–1347. Washington, D.C.: U.S. Office of Education.

Sievers, Eduard. 1876. *Grundzüge der Lautphysiologie.* Leipzig: Breitkopf und Härtel.

Sledd, James. 1966. "Breaking, Umlaut, and the Southern Drawl." *Language* 42:18–41.

Stewart, William A. 1967. "Sociolinguistic Factors in the History of American Negro Dialects." *Florida FL Reporter*, vol. 5, no. 2, pp. 11, 22, 24, 26. Reprinted in Wolfram and Clarke 1971:74–89.

———. 1968. "Continuity and Change in American Negro Dialects." *Florida FL Reporter*, vol. 6, no. 1, pp. 3–4, 14–16, 18.

Stockwell, Robert P. 1959. "Structural Dialectology: A Proposal." *American Speech* 34:258–68. Reprinted in Allen and Underwood 1971:314–23.

Trager, George L., and Smith, Henry Lee. 1951. *An Outline of English Structure.* Washington, D.C.: American Council of Learned Societies.

Toike, Rudolph C. 1971. "Overall Pattern and Generative Phonology." In Allen and Underwood 1971:324–42.

Turner, Lorenzo D. 1948. *Africanisms in the Gullah Dialect.* Chicago: University of Chicago Press.

Underwood, Gary N. 1976. "American English Dialectology: Alternatives for the Southwest." *International Journal of the Sociology of Language* 2:19–40.

Wakelin, Martyn F. 1972. *English Dialects: An Introduction.* London: Athlone Press.

Weinreich, Uriel. 1954. "Is a Structural Dialectology Possible?" *Word* 10:388–400. Reprinted in Allen and Underwood 1971:300–13.

Wenker, Georg. 1877. *Das rheinische Platt.* Dusseldorf: n.p.

Winteler, Jost. 1876. *Die Kerenzer Mundart des Kantons Glarus.* Leipzig and Heidelberg: C. F. Winter.

Wolfram, Walter A. 1969. *A Sociolinguistic Description of Detroit Negro Speech.* Washington, D.C.: Center for Applied Linguistics.

———. 1971. "Black-White Speech Differences Revisited." In Wolfram and Clarke 1971:139–61.

———. 1974a. "The Relationship of White Southern Speech to Vernacular Black English." *Language* 50:498–527.

———. 1974b. *Sociolinguistic Aspects of Assimilation: Puerto Rican English in New York*

*City*. Washington, D.C.: Center for Applied Linguistics.

———, and Christian, Donna. 1976. *Appalachian Speech*. Washington, D.C.: Center for Applied Linguistics.

———, and Clarke, Nona H. 1971. *Black-White Speech Relationships*. Washington, D.C.: Center for Applied Linguistics.

———, and Fasold, Ralph. 1974. *The Study of Social Dialects in American English*. Washington, D.C.: Center for Applied Linguistics.

Wright, Joseph. 1898–1905. *English Dialect Dictionary*. 6 vols. Oxford: Oxford University Press.

# Index

45920045